NOT PEACE BUT A SWORD

"All of Christ's faithful,
whatever be the conditions, duties,
and circumstances of their lives,
will grow in holiness day by day
through these very situations..."

Vatican II: Constitution on the Church, 41

FELICITY O'BRIEN

NOT PEACE
BUT A SWORD

John Henry Newman

 St Paul Publications

Acknowledgement

I would like to express my deep gratitude to Father Peter Gumpel, SJ, Relator for the Cause of Cardinal Newman, for taking the time and trouble to kindly read the manuscript for this book, and for his helpful comments and advice. I am also grateful to Fr Gumpel for allowing me access to the *Copia Publica* of documents relating to the Cause. Responsibility for any errors or inaccuracies must now lie with the author.

Felicity O'Brien

St Paul Publications
Middlegreen, Slough SL3 6BT, England

Copyright © St Paul Publications 1990
Printed by Dotesios Printers Ltd, Trowbridge
Cover by Mary Lou Winters
ISBN 085439 327 7

St Paul Publications is an activity of the priests and brothers of the Society of St Paul who promote the Gospel through the media of social communication

In affectionate memory of
Cardinal John Carmel Heenan
Archbishop of Westminster 1963-1975

Notes

References and sources of quotations are given at the end of each chapter. Abbreviations have been kept to a minimum:

CP   =   *Copia Publica*
LD   =   *Letters and Diaries of John Henry Newman*
PPS =   *Parochial and Plain Sermons*

The original punctuation has been kept in the quotations.

Contents

Section I

A Path to Truth

1

"Myself and my Creator"

John Henry Newman seems so much a part of the late 20th century that one could be forgiven for forgetting that the historical context of his life and work was the very different world of the 19th century. For fifty-three years of his life, Queen Victoria was the reigning monarch in the United Kingdom — and became Empress of India in 1876. Among Newman's contemporaries were Napoleon III, Abraham Lincoln, Garibaldi, Gladstone and Disraeli. The literary scene included Wordsworth, Longfellow and Tennyson; Jane Austin, the Brontës and Charles Dickens.

It was a century which still saw children sweeping chimneys, going down mines and working in factories. Education was something for the 'better off': not until 1870 was an elementary education made available to all British children, by Forster's Education Act. In the 1830's only about two-thirds of men and one-third of women could write their names.

Living conditions for many families were appalling and squalid in the extreme. When cholera arrived in London in 1830 there was every fear that it would prove as devastating as the Great Plague. Local boards of health were set up around the country and a central board in London. Reports showed conditions in towns and cities which threatened the breakdown of civilized society.

It was the century of the Crimean War and the American Civil War, and 1848 saw revolutionary movements in many European countries.

Marx and Engels produced their Communist Manifesto; Florence Nightingale became a legendary figure for her work during the Crimean War; David Livingstone explored the African interior; Charles Darwin published his *Origin of Species*; Lister and Pasteur were responsible for notable advances in the medical field. And in a then obscure spot in the Pyrenees the pilgrimage centre of Lourdes was born when a young girl called Bernadette claimed to see visions of a beautiful lady who spoke of herself as the Immaculate Conception.

Roman Catholics in Britain were beginning to emerge from the icy winter they had passed through under the severe penal laws enacted against them following the Reformation. Much prejudice still remained and to join their number was to invite ostracization from one's family and friends. The Catholic Emancipation Act in 1829 and the restoration of the Roman Catholic Hierarchy in England and Wales in 1850 by the Holy See, were signs of the thaw but also gave rise to evidence of the widespread prejudice, hostility and suspicion that existed.

The numbers of Catholics grew rapidly because of the immigration of Irish Catholics during the potato famine, an influx of foreign missionaries, and by conversions among highly educated Oxford men. The resulting mix was hardly homogeneous and the 'old' Catholics whose families had lived in England since the Reformation times were faced with many changes in attitudes and practices.

John Henry Newman's life spanned almost the entire century. He was born on 21 February 1801, the first of his parents' six children. The London Stock Exchange now stands where the house in which he was born and the church of St Benet Fink where he was baptised on 9 April, once stood. His father, John Newman, whose family came from Cambridgeshire, was a banker in the City of London; his mother, Jemima Fourdrinier, came from a French Protestant, Huguenot, family who settled in England after the revocation of the Edict of Nantes. They were members of the Established Church, and the Bible was much read at home. It was his grandmother in particular who led the young John Henry to a great love of the Scriptures and he always remembered her with affectionate gratitude.

He enjoyed a happy childhood with the brothers and sisters who followed him: Charles, Harriett, Francis, Jemima and Mary. He especially loved the family's country home of Grey Court House, at Ham, near Richmond. Details of the house remained impressed on his mind long after the family had ceased going there.

He was an intellectually bright child. His

schooling began at the age of seven when he was sent to a private boarding school in Ealing. Dr George Nicholas, who ran the school, said that no boy had progressed so quickly up the school as the young John Henry Newman. Schoolboy activities included being the leader of a boys' club; editing a number of magazines; writing a mock drama and a burlesque opera. He rarely played actual games, but he liked flying kites, walking, riding and boating. He loved music and learnt to play the violin.

He was an imaginative child and recalled in later years that he had wished the Arabian Tales were true: "My imagination ran on unknown influences, on magical powers, and talismans . . . I thought life might be a dream, or I an Angel, and all this world a deception, my fellow-angels by a playful device concealing themselves from me, and deceiving me with the semblance of a material world."[1]

In a sense, this way of thinking presages his later conviction that the material world was a "sacrament" of the immensely more important and real, invisible world. But this development was not to take place until he had been through a personal crisis and a conversion experience at the end of his school years.

At the age of fourteen he read Tom Paine's *Tracts*[2] *against the Old Testament* and enjoyed thinking about the objections they contained. Some of the Essays by the atheistic philosopher, David Hume, and a number of French verses against the immortality of the

14

soul also influenced him. Then, in 1816, a major problem faced the family. John Newman's bank failed because of the inflation which followed the Napoleonic Wars. The depositors were paid their money, but the Newmans' London home had to be let and the family moved to Alton in Hampshire where John Newman became the manager of a brewery. John Henry had completed the course of studies at Ealing but, because of the family's difficulties, he remained with his brother at the school during the summer months while his family moved to Alton.

During that summer John Henry suffered from a fever. It became the occasion of the beginning of a conversion experience which lasted from August to December 1816. During his illness, a young Evangelical clergyman, Walter Mayers, who taught at the school, spoke to him about God's mercy and forgiveness and lent him some books which had a profound effect on him. Later, he wrote: "I fell under the influences of a definite creed, and received into my intellect impressions of dogma, which, through God's mercy, have never been effaced or obscured."[3]

After reading a book by William Romaine,[4] he felt an inner certainty that his conversion was forever and that he was "elected to eternal glory". The thought, as far as he could recollect, did not make him careless in trying to serve God, and it remained a strong conviction for about six years. He considered that this experience further confirmed him in his

"mistrust of the reality of material pheno-
mena." It made him "rest in the thought of
two and two only supreme and luminously
self-evident beings, myself and my Creator."[5]
He did not think about the implication of the
doctrine of predestination, namely that some
were predestined not to be saved; he thought
only of others being "passed over" and of
himself having been shown great mercy. He
later regarded the doctrine of predestination as
"detestable".

Two works which particularly influenced him
at this time were Thomas Scott's *The Force of
Truth*[6] and Joseph Milner's *History of the
Church of Christ*.[7] He said of Scott: "He
followed truth wherever it led him . . ." That
description could equally be applied to Newman
himself. It was from Scott, whose beliefs had
moved from Unitarianism to Trinitarianism,
that Newman learnt to have a deep love for the
doctrine of the Trinity. Scott had "planted deep
in my mind that fundamental truth of religion". Newman liked the "minutely practical
character" of Scott's writings and his "bold un-
worldliness and vigorous independence of
mind". Two particular sayings of Scott remained firmly in Newman's mind: "Holiness before
peace" and "Growth is the only evidence of
life".[8] The two sayings provide almost a
blueprint for Newman's life and work.

Milner's work gave Newman a great love for
the Fathers of the Church, who would eventually be a major influence in his conversion to
Roman Catholicism. In their writings Newman

saw the religion of the early Christians, the primitive Church. While reading Milner's work he also read Newton's work, *On the Prophecies*,[9] and became completely convinced that the Pope was the Antichrist. This conviction, he said, stained his imagination up until 1843 even though it had been "obliterated" earlier in his reason and judgement.

Following his conversion experience, he felt he should keep his distance from worldly pleasures which might draw him away from his newly found religious convictions. But it was not simply a matter of turning from worldly pleasures and amusements: it was a turning more and more towards God. From 1816 he felt within himself a growing conviction that the path he would be called to follow in life would require him to be celibate. At first the thought came and went but after 1829 it remained with him. He felt drawn to work as a missionary. This growing conviction with regard to celibacy strengthened his "feeling of separation from the visible world".[10]

On 14 December 1816, Newman went with his father to Oxford where he was admitted to Trinity College. However, it was not possible for him to take up residence until the following June, so he returned to Alton with his father.

Bishop William Beveridge's book *Private Thoughts*[11] was among his reading in the months of waiting to go up to Oxford. It encouraged his piety and he tried his hand at writing sermons like Beveridge. Many years later Newman

17

said that no book had been more dear to him.

Newman's early life at university was not easy. He was studious and industrious. His fellow students, for the most part, were not. He much preferred peace and quiet to their rowdy activities where drinking was much featured. The fact that he played the violin was considered to be a subject for mirth. When he was invited to play at one student party, he went along but quickly realised he was to be the butt of their humour and refused to play. Their attempts to get him drunk fared no better: he drank a few glasses of wine and then left the party. His firmness won in the end and he was no longer pestered to attend wine parties.

On his arrival at the university Newman had made friends with John William Bowden and their undergraduate years often found them studying together or going for walks and boating. Newman still enjoyed music, attending concerts and joining a small orchestra. Nevertheless, the hours of study took their toll and he sometimes fell asleep over his books or suffered from faintness.

At the end of his first year at university, Newman won a Trinity College scholarship which was worth the then considerable sum of £60 a year over the next nine years.

With the end of the first year also came the annual college Communion. Newman was appalled to find that those who attended this saw nothing wrong with getting drunk at the breakfast that followed. His reverence for the Sacrament was great although he had not

18

yet come to believe in the "Real Presence".

When he came to his final examinations in 1820, Newman was expected to do very well. However, he was concerned that success might cause him to be proud and ambitious in worldly matters, and prayed that he would fail rather than commit sin. Nevertheless, he was anxious not to let down his parents and others who thought he would gain Honours in the exams although he was two years younger than most entrants. In the end, overwork and anxiety led to his nerves getting the better of him in the exams. When the results came out, his name was among those described somewhat contemptuously as "under-the-line". It was a bare pass but he regarded it as both a chastisement for past offences and a preventive for the future. For a while Newman had been uncertain about his future: a career in Law held its attractions and his father had considered that he should follow that path. However, his poor exam results more or less precluded any further thought of a Law career, and it was not long before he turned to the idea of dedicating his life to God and being ordained.

In 1821 his father was declared bankrupt, the Alton brewery having failed. It meant that family possessions had to be sold. Newman did his best to keep the bankruptcy secret for the sake of his father whom he regarded as having worked and exhausted himself for his family.

With the earlier Trinity scholarship and by taking pupils, Newman was able to stay at university himself and pay for his younger brother, Frank, to go there as well. It was not easy and there were occasions when Newman was in considerable financial difficulty. Frank tended to be obstinate and without humour, and Newman found his patience sorely tried at times. However, in later years, when he apologized to his brother for his former bad temper, Frank said he could not remember any such occasions and regarded him as kind and generous in those years.

Newman's father had been none too happy with his conversion to Evangelicalism. Frank had been much influenced by the same Evangelical clergyman as John Henry, but had adopted a more intransigent approach to his religion, refusing on one occasion to copy a letter on the Sabbath. John Henry was asked for his opinion and had backed him up. It had caused a family row and afterwards he regarded himself as having been "sadly deficient in meekness, long suffering, patience and filial obedience". He added: "With God's assistance, I will redeem my character".[12]

His father warned him that extreme religious fervour could weaken the mind and assured him that no one's principles could be firmly established at the age of twenty. John Henry wrote in his journal:

> O God, grant me to pray earnestly against any delusive heat, or fanatic fancy, or proud imagination of fancied superiority, or uncharitable zeal. Make me and keep me humble and teachable, modest and cautious.[13]

20

Newman was endeavouring to lead a truly Christian life. It was certainly a life of prayer, awareness of God's presence, meditation, thanksgiving, petitions for friends and for humankind in general, reading of the Scriptures, and examining his conscience as a means of discovering and correcting his faults. He was concerned not only about bad temper but also about pride, vanity and sexual temptations. Some years later, he spoke about saints and the temptations they face and overcome:

> He grows up, and he has just the same temptations as others, perhaps more violent ones. Men of the world, carnal men, unbelieving men, do not believe that the temptations which they themselves experience, and to which they yield, can be overcome. They reason themselves into the notion that to sin is their very nature and, therefore, is no fault of theirs; that is, they deny the existence of sin.[14]

Newman's views on these matters were clearly not those of men of the world.

In April 1822, he stood for a Fellowship at Oriel College, Oxford. He obviously hoped to be elected but tried to temper his hopes with the likely reality that he would not succeed at the first attempt. It was a prestigious position. He was also concerned that success might feed pride and ambition. He considered that he lacked the humility and spirituality to be successful without it being harmful to him:

> There is every reason for thinking I shall not succeed in my object, and I seem to see it would

21

not be good for me — but my evil heart boils over with vain-glorious anticipations of success.[15]

In the February before his election as a Fellow, as his birthday came round, Newman wrote:

Lord, take anything, everything away, if I may not purchase grace without the sacrifice. Thou knowest my heart — I am in Thy Presence. Thou seest how fondly, and I fear idolatrously, my affections are set on succeeding at Oriel. Take all hope away, stop not an instant, O my God, if so doing will gain me Thy Spirit.[16]

It was the sort of heartfelt, impetuous prayer that he liked to make in his youth but which, in more mature years, he doubted he would be able to make in exactly the same way without "some vast and extraordinary grant of grace."[17] He had been bold, he said, but with increasing experience he was "able to count the cost, better than I did, of being brave for Thy sake, and therefore I shrink from sacrifices."[18]

With his tutor's encouragement, Newman passed successfully through the five-day examination and was elected a Fellow of Oriel on 12 April 1822. He noted in his journal: "I have this morning been elected Fellow of Oriel. Thank God, thank God."[19] His delight was reflected in the speed with which he raced down the stairs and over to Oriel College on being given the news of his success. This success also opened up a theological career in which Newman would continue to develop spiritually and intellectually.

At first he was extremely shy in the company of so many distinguished people, and scarcely said a word in the common room. The other Fellows tried, in vain, to unlock his tongue. Of those early years at Oriel, he wrote: ". . . though proud of my college, I was not at home there. I was very much alone, and I used often to take my daily walk by myself."[20]

There was, he said, no one to whom he could really open his heart. However, it was during this period that he made friends with Edward Pusey who, like Newman, was to be a leader of the Oxford Movement but, unlike him, he would remain in the Church of England.

On 13 June 1824 — Trinity Sunday — Newman was ordained a deacon in the Church of England. The ceremony took place in Christ Church cathedral. He felt over-awed and unworthy to be a minister of Christ. He wrote:

> I am thine, O Lord; I seem quite dizzy, and cannot altogether believe and understand it. At first, after the hands were laid on me, my heart shuddered within me; the words "for ever" are so terrible. It was hardly a godly feeling which made me feel melancholy at the idea of giving up all for God. At times indeed my heart burnt within me, particularly during the singing of the *Veni Creator*. Yet, Lord, I ask not for comfort in comparison of sanctification . . . I feel as a man thrown suddenly into deep water.[21]

The next day he wrote: "I have the responsibility for souls on me to the day of my death . . .,"[22] and wept at the thought of his own sinfulness.

Shortly after his ordination he called at Church Missionary House in London to enquire about the possibility of being accepted for missionary work. He was assured that "weakness of voice, shortness of sight, want of eloquence"[23] were not impediments to his acceptance. His scholastic achievements were much needed and the posts he could fill did not require a strong constitution. However, his father's death on 3 October 1824 left him the only member of the family earning an income, and so missionary work seemed somewhat remote for the time being.

Before ordination he had accepted the curacy of St Clement's, a parish of some 1500 people. The Rector there was elderly and infirm which left Newman with much to do in the parish. He began his ministry by visiting each house. Throughout the two years he was there he spent much time visiting the sick and dying and giving what material assistance he could although his own financial position was none too bright. During his ministry he gathered nearly one hundred children to form a Sunday school. He also managed to raise enough contributions to pay for a new church. The path of parochial life was not always smooth and at one point he had a dispute with the official singers at the church and they departed. Newman reported in a letter: "We now sing *en masse*."

While working in St Clement's parish,

Newman began to move from the Evangelical beliefs he had firmly held since his conversion experience at the age of fifteen.

Notes

[1] *Apologia*, p. 29.
[2] Tom Paine (1737–1809). Born in Norfolk, England, he went to America in 1774 where he supported the colonists in the War of Independence. He returned to England in 1787, and published the first part of his popular work *The Rights of Man* in 1791 and the second part the following year. He supported the French Revolution and represented Calais in the French National Convention. He ridiculed Christian beliefs and institutions as superstition.
[3] *Apologia*, p. 31.
[4] William Romaine (1714–1795). A Calvinist preacher.
[5] *Apologia*, p. 31.
[6] Thomas Scott (1747–1821). Rector of Aston Sandford, Buckinghamshire, England, from 1801. His weekly commentary on the Bible, issued from 1788 to 1792, was widely circulated.
[7] Joseph Milner (1744–1797). An Evangelical divine.
[8] *Apologia*, p. 32.
[9] Thomas Newton. Bishop of Bristol from 1761–1782.
[10] *Apologia*, p. 34.
[11] William Beveridge (1637–1708). Bishop of St Asaph, in Wales, 1704–1708.
[12] *Autobiographical Writings*, p. 176.
[13] Ibid., p. 179.
[14] *Discourses to Mixed Congregations*, No. V, pp. 97–98.
[15] *Autobiographical Writings*, p. 178.
[16] Ibid., p. 183.
[17] Ibid., p. 250.
[18] Ibid., p. 251.
[19] Ibid., p. 186.
[20] *Apologia*, p. 40.
[21] *Autobiographical Writings*, p. 200.
[22] Ibid., p. 201.
[23] Ibid., p. 201.

2

Towards the Light

When Newman was working at St Clement's, Edward Hawkins was Vicar of St Mary's University Church in Oxford, and he gave Newman a copy of Sumner's *Treatise on Apostolical Preaching*.[1] From this, Newman said he learnt to "give up my remaining Calvinism, and to receive the doctrine of Baptismal Regeneration."[2] Practical experience in his parish also led him away from Calvinism as he saw many people who were "inconsistent" regarding important points but who could not be said to be without grace.

From Hawkins, Newman also learnt the doctrine of Tradition:

> He lays down a proposition, self-evident as soon as stated, to those who have at all examined the structure of Scripture, viz. that the sacred text was never intended to teach doctrine, but only to prove it, and that, if we would learn doctrine, we must have recourse to the formularies of the Church; for instance to the Catechism, and to the Creeds.[3]

It was a view which Newman regarded as having opened up for him a "large field of thought".

Around this time, Newman was also led to

hold "freer views" about the inspiration of Scripture than were commonly held then in the Church of England. And it was while walking round Christ Church meadow that Newman learnt from William James, another Fellow of Oriel, the doctrine of Apostolic Succession.

Bishop Butler's *Analogy*[4] proved to be another major influence on Newman with its "inculcation of a visible Church, the oracle of truth and a pattern of sanctity, of the duties of external religion, and of the historical character of revelation".[5] This work drew Newman to see creation as a "sacrament" of the greater, invisible reality. He was also struck by Butler's teaching that "probability is the guide to life". However, he was concerned that taken to its extreme form this teaching could result in praying: "O God, if there is a God, save my soul, if I have a soul", because it tended to destroy certainty, making every conclusion doubtful and truth no more than opinion safe to profess but impossible to embrace with complete inner assent. John Keble, in his *Christian Year*,[6] reinforced for Newman these two aspects of Butler's work. Keble went some way in Newman's estimation to resolving the problem concerning probability by saying that faith and love gave probability a force which it did not have in itself. But Newman felt Keble's solution was still not reaching the fundamental difficulty regarding "probability", and set out to develop it further, by saying in effect that the sheer weight and quality of a number of probabilities could be such when taken together as to make for absolute certitude, that is, absolute inner conviction. It involved private judgement but it was one that resulted from a conscientious approach with a sense of duty rather than mere personal fancy formed arbitrarily.

The prayerful, diligent nature of Newman's own search for truth can be seen in his writings in this period. In August 1824 he wrote:

> Lately I have been thinking much on the subject of grace, regeneration etc. and reading Sumner's *Apostolical Preaching*, which Hawkins has given me. Sumner's book threatens to drive me either into Calvinism, or baptismal regeneration, and I wish to steer clear of both, at least in preaching. I am always slow in deciding a question; last night I was so distressed and low about it, that a slight roughness from someone nearly brought me to tears, and the thought even struck me I must leave the Church. I have been praying about it before I rose this morning, and I do not know what will be the end of it. I think I really desire the truth, and would embrace it wherever I found it.[7]

Five months later, he was writing:

> I think, I am not certain, I must give up the doctrine of imputed righteousness and that of regeneration as apart from baptism.[9]

And a month later:

> The necessity of composing sermons has obliged me to systematize and complete my ideas on many subjects — on several questions, however (those connected with regeneration) though I have thought much, and (I hope) prayed

28

much, yet I hardly dare say confidently that my change of opinion has brought me nearer to the truth.[9]

His parish work left him little time for the development of his spiritual life, for personal devotions and for studying the Scriptures. However, he said that he prayed constantly as he walked and went about his work. His comment regarding the observance of the Sabbath no doubt brings wry smiles to the faces of all clergy:

> I confess I waver very much, but to a clergyman, whose hands are full of business on Sunday it is personally a question of comparatively small importance.[10]

In March 1825 he became Vice-Principal at Alban Hall, Oxford, where Dr Whately, later Protestant Archbishop of Dublin, was Principal. He had taken the young Newman in hand when he was a new, shy Fellow of Oriel. He taught Newman to see the Church as a "substantive body" and to fix in him "anti-Erastian views of Church polity, which were one of the most prominent features of the Tractarian Movement."[11]

On 29 May, the Feast of Pentecost, Newman was ordained a priest in the Church of England. The following August saw him celebrating Communion for the first time. It was also the occasion of the First Communion of his sisters, Mary and Jemima. He dearly loved all three of his sisters, so much so that he feared that they would be taken from him before long.

In 1826 Newman became a tutor at Oriel College, and in order to devote himself adequately to this he gave up St Clement's and Alban Hall. At the latter, the Principal offered to raise his salary to equal that which he would be getting as a college tutor, in order to keep him at Alban Hall, but Newman turned it down.

In the same year Newman met Richard Hurrell Froude who was to become another close friend. Froude, who was not, of course, a Roman Catholic, led Newman to develop an admiration for the Church of Rome, a belief in the Real Presence of Christ in the Eucharist, and the idea of devotion to the Blessed Virgin, whom Froude saw as the great pattern for virginity which he held in highest esteem.

As a tutor, Newman took seriously the university statute that tutors should give their pupils moral guidance and religious instruction, teaching them the doctrine of reliable authors. This was a generally neglected aspect of the tutors' work, but Newman saw it as being of the first importance and was determined that he would care for his pupils' spiritual good, and if he found there were no opportunities to do this he would seriously question whether he should continue as a tutor.

Newman's efforts to raise the religious awareness and moral attitudes in the college made him unpopular with some, but eventually he won respect. And those whom he tutored soon came to appreciate that he genuinely cared for their welfare.

One of his former undergraduates, James

Anthony Froude, later recalled what Newman had been like with them:

> He seemed always to be better informed on common topics of conversation than anyone else who was present. He was never condescending with us, never didactic or authoritative; but what he said carried conviction along with it. When we were wrong he knew why we were wrong, and excused our mistakes to ourselves while he set us right. Perhaps his supreme merit as a teacher was that he never tried to be witty or to say striking things. Ironical he could be, but not ill-natured. Not a malicious anecdote was ever heard from him. Prosy he could not be. He was lightness itself — the lightness of elastic strength, and he was interesting because he never talked for talking's sake, but because he had something real to say.
> . . . Personal admiration, of course, inclined us to look to him as a guide in matters of religion. No one who heard his sermons in those days can ever forget them.[12]

In 1827 he became ill from fatigue and worry. At the college there was concern over the election for a new Provost for Oriel. But, even more, Newman had been busy preparing himself for his newly appointed task of examiner. On the family side of things, he was desperately worried at the failure of his aunt's school which had left her with debts of around £700. For a while, it had seemed that he might have to try and find all the money himself, in addition to paying for a house for his family in Brighton.

He had recovered in time for Christmas and joined his family in Brighton for the festivities.

However, on 5 January 1828, his sister, Mary, died suddenly at the age of nineteen. It was a bitter blow for Newman, the most painful that he had yet had to bear in his life. Just as his illness and the financial problems of his father in 1816 had been the initial setting for the first major development in his spiritual life, so his illness in the autumn of 1827 and the death of his sister at the beginning of 1828 were the prelude to another profound development in his way of thinking.

He was now conscious of having begun to prefer intellectual excellence to moral excellence. He had also become aware that he had been drifting into liberalism, with its views of one opinion being as good as another and there being no such thing as objective religious truth. His illness, Mary's death, and not long after that the death of Walter Mayers, who had had such an influence on him early on, reinforced Newman's striving for holiness, and his views on the passing nature of this world. These views and his love for his sister can be seen in a letter he wrote to Jemima, four months after Mary's death. He had been out riding, and said: "Dear Mary seems embodied in every tree and hid behind every hill. What a veil and curtain the world of sense is! beautiful but still a veil!"[13]

In 1828 Newman was appointed Vicar of St Mary's University Church, replacing Dr Hawkins who had become Provost of Oriel College. In the same year, Newman began to read through the Church Fathers in chronological order. This study was to raise considerable

32

alarm in Newman's mind because he could see similarities between the beginnings of Arianism and the growing "liberal" spirit in the Church of England: the questioning of revealed truths which led into heresy.

In 1829, following disagreements with the Provost about the tutorial system which he and two other tutors considered did not provide opportunities for the proper pastoral care of students, Newman resigned as a tutor. This meant that he had more time to devote to the study of the Church Fathers. He was asked to write a book about the Council of Nicea, for a series on early Church Councils, and he readily agreed. However, it was not long before he had moved back, by way of introduction, into pre-Nicene history and in particular to the Church of Alexandria where Athanasius had been the champion of truth against Arianism. The result was that in some 400 pages the actual Council of Nicea made its appearance for about twenty pages. The book was not suitable for the planned appearance in the series but was published separately, under the title: *The Arians of the Fourth Century*.

In the Church Fathers Newman found something of his own long-held ideas. He saw in them the "sacramental" view of the material world that he himself cherished; that "the exterior world, physical and historical, was but the outward manifestation of realities greater than itself".[14] He saw Judaism and Paganism as an outer framework "which concealed yet suggested the living truth";[15] the framework

had not been intended to last. Change had
come slowly but steadily with one disclosure
following another until the whole was revealed.

> And thus room was made for the anticipation
> of further and deeper disclosures of truths still
> under the veil of the letter, and in their season
> to be revealed. The visible world remains without
> its divine interpretation; Holy Church in her
> sacraments and her hierarchical appointments,
> will remain even to the end of the world, only
> a symbol of those heavenly facts which fill
> eternity. Her mysteries are but the expressions in
> human language of truths to which the human
> mind is unequal.[16]

Newman's beliefs regarding angels, he ascribed to the Alexandrian school and the
early Christian Church. His views were along
the lines of Francis Thompson's poem, "In
No Strange Land", which includes the verse:

> The angels keep their ancient places;
> Turn but a stone, and start a wing!
> Tis ye, 'tis your estranged faces,
> That miss the many splendoured thing.

In a sermon for the feast of St Michael,
Newman wrote: "Every breath of air and ray
of light and heat, every beautiful prospect is,
as it were, the skirts of their garments, the
waving of the robes of those whose faces see
God."[17]

It is not perhaps the language with which
many late 20th century scholarly devotees of
Newman would be happiest, but it is still
Newman and evidence of his vital awareness of
the invisible world.

In December 1832 Newman joined Richard Hurrell Froude and the latter's father on a visit to the Mediterranean. They sailed from Falmouth on 8 December and travelled to Spain, Gibraltar, Algiers, Corfu, Zante and Patras, Malta, Sicily, Naples and Rome where they arrived on 2 March 1833. Naples did not appeal in the least to Newman — and a pickpocket nearly got the better of him — but he did find Salerno and Amalfi beautiful. He was bowled over by the city of Rome with its wealth of art and architecture. It even scored over his beloved Oxford in his estimation. But it was Sicily that held a special fascination for him. When the Froudes returned to England, Newman decided to remain behind and visit Sicily at a leisurely pace on his own. He went back to Naples to prepare for the journey and also engaged a servant, Gennaro, to travel with him. They sailed from Naples on 19 April and arrived in Messina two days later. Newman suffered from sea-sickness during the voyage. From Messina they set out on a tour of the island which would have been a challenge to a seasoned traveller at that time, let alone an Oxford don inexperienced in such adventures. The toughness of the journeying is abundantly clear from Newman's subsequent writings. Shortly before he became ill with a fever which was widespread and causing many deaths, he had spent a night in an open boat, followed by a thirty-two mile journey by mule to Catania.

We set forward on mules for Catania with the belief that the distance was twenty-two miles. By the time it grew dusk we had gone fourteen miles, and descended to the water's side; when to our dismay we learned we had eighteen miles before us, three rivers to ford or ferry, a deep sand to traverse for half the way, and the danger of being plundered. To complete the whole, when we got to the most suspicious part of our journey our guide lost his way. . . We got to Catania between eleven and twelve at night. The sun had been broiling during the day — the night was damp.[18]

When he became ill, serious as it was, he was convinced that he would not die, because God had some special work for him in England. During his illness, he accused himself of pride and self-will, of being a hollow person, having little love and little in the way of self-denial. The one favourable point he could find in himself was that he had not "sinned against the light".[19] Now he was determined to obey the will of God.

On 13 June, Newman sailed from Palermo towards Marseilles, en route for England. During the journey, when the ship lay becalmed in the straits of Bonifacio, Newman wrote the poem, *The Pillar of the Cloud*, which became better known as the well-loved hymn *Lead, kindly Light*. It was an outpouring of his soul as he gently sank into the recognition of his own human nothingness and surrendered himself to the infinite wisdom and mercy of God. It was no sudden conversion. He had been trying to come closer to Christ, to search for religious truth; he had been anxious not to be affected by pride and worldly, vain ambition. But this third major religious experience during his illness in Sicily led him to pour out even more fervently his longing for the light of Christ to grow stronger in his life, to lead him as the pillar of cloud had led God's people through the desert:

"Lead, kindly Light, amid the
    encircling gloom,
Lead Thou me on . . .
I was not ever thus nor didst I pray
    that Thou
shouldst lead me on . . .
Pride ruled my will; remember not
    past years."[20]

Newman arrived back home in England on 9 July 1833 and on the 14th of that month John Keble preached his sermon on "National Apostasy". Newman came to regard this as the beginning of the Oxford Movement, of which he was to become the unofficial leader.

Notes

[1] John Bird Sumner (1780–1862). Archbishop of Canterbury from 1848–1862.
[2] *Apologia*, p. 35.
[3] Ibid., p. 35.
[4] Joseph Butler (1692–1752). Became Bishop of Durham in 1750 after having been Bishop of Bristol since 1738. His *Analogy of Natural and Revealed Religion* was published in 1736.
[5] *Apologia*, p. 36.
[6] *The Christian Year* was a collection of poems for Sundays and holy days throughout the Church's year. It was published in 1827.

[7] *Autobiographical Writings*, p. 202.
[8] Ibid., p. 203.
[9] Ibid., p. 204.
[10] Ibid., p. 205.
[11] *Apologia*, p. 37.
[12] J. A. Froude, *Short Studies on Great Subjects*, Vol. IV, Longmans, Green and Co., London, 1899, pp. 282–283.
[13] Letter to his sister, Jemima, 10/5/1828. *Letters*, edited by Stanford and Spark, p. 48.
[14] *Apologia*, p. 49.
[15] Ibid., p. 49.
[16] Ibid., pp. 49–50.
[17] Ibid., p. 50.
[18] *Autobiographical Writings*, p. 116.
[19] Ibid., p. 125.
[20] *Verses on Various Occasions*, No. 84 (and in numerous hymn books).

3

"Lead Thou me on"

The early 19th century saw several attempts to revitalize the Church of England but, of these, the Oxford Movement was the best known and most effective. It gave rise to important and long-term developments in the attitude towards the Church and in its worship; it also gave rise to divisions and suspicions between its supporters and promoters and those who feared that it was much too orientated towards Rome.

In the 18th and 19th centuries many changes were needed in both secular and religious spheres. But those who advocated any change were severely hampered by the widespread fear that change could breed discontent and the destruction of the status quo. This fear had become even more marked when the initial aura of optimism and liberation of the French Revolution in the 18th century had quickly turned to terror and the breakdown of law and order. In England, the Church was seen as an important means of keeping people in their respective places. It was seen as a stabilizing influence in society. The idea of Church and State being linked together was widely accepted. However, there was little, if any, thought of the Church as a spiritual entity founded by Christ, with bishops as successors of the Apostles. Nor was there sufficient thought given to its mission or authority. The Oxford Movement aimed to rectify this.

Its leaders and followers were concerned at the way in which Governments could interfere in church affairs, a concern which was increased by the moves afoot to admit people into Parliament who were not members of the Church of England. A particular source of concern had been the Irish Church Act of 1833, which rearranged certain boundaries of Sees in Ireland. It was just such secular interference which those who formed and supported the Oxford Movement feared and resented. This Irish question had prompted Keble's sermon.

The leaders of the Movement in its early days were Fellows of Oriel College in Oxford. Along with Newman there was John Keble, Edward Pusey and Richard Hurrell Froude. They wanted to restore to the Church of England a real sense of its divine origin and mission. They saw it endangered from within and without. Within, there were the problems of Church subordination to State with bishops being drawn into politics and away from their true episcopal role and the subsequent detrimental effect this had on the Church at all levels; of nominalism which was hostile to dogmatic statements and creeds, regarding them as passing and changeable expressions of belief; of rationalism which destroyed any religious "enthusiasm" or sense of mystery — everything was reduced to what was "reasonable"; and the type of Evangelicalism which saw little importance in the structures of the Church and its formal prayer life. Threats to the Church from outside it came from the general spirit of the times which included a preoccupation with material things to the detriment of the spiritual, and the rejection of religious values and authority.

Newman saw in the Oxford Movement that work which he had felt God wanted him to do in England, at the time when he was seriously ill and in danger of death from fever in Sicily.

> I had the consciousness that I was employed in that work which I had been dreaming about, and which I felt to be so momentous and inspiring. I had supreme confidence in our cause; we were upholding that primitive Christianity which was delivered for all time by the early teachers of the Church and which was registered and attested in the Anglican formularies and by the Anglican divines. That ancient religion had well nigh faded away out of the land, through the political changes in the last 150 years, and it must be restored.[1]

His confidence in the aims of the Movement were based on three propositions: the principle of dogma; the belief in "a visible church with sacraments and rites which are channels of invisible grace"; and opposition to the Church of Rome.[2]

Newman's sermons at that time were the most powerful force in the Oxford Movement, and his fame as a preacher was widespread. He also wrote many of the *Tracts for the Times*, which promoted the views of the Movement. The sermons were eventually published in the eight volumes of *Parochial and Plain Sermons*, covering the period 1825–1843; and *University Sermons*, a one-volume collection of Newman's fifteen sermons before the university, were from the same period.

The Tracts written by Newman and other leaders of the Oxford Movement, causing them to become known as "Tractarians", were based on the article of the Creed: "I believe in one Catholic and Apostolic Church." They set out to revive ideas about the Church, the sacraments, the priesthood and piety in general which had been forgotten. The writers did not see themselves as preaching something new but rather as going back to original views of the Church before the Reformation, and to practices contained in the Book of Common Prayer which were ordered by law but had been ignored or forgotten. However, the attitude of the Tractarians towards rites and institutions and, above all, their concentration on Apostolic Succession, aroused the suspicions of many that they were heading Romewards and that possibly some of them might already be Roman Catholic, even Jesuits. The suspicions regarding the direction being taken by the Tractarians seemed justified when some of the leaders and supporters of the Movement began leaving the Church of England for Rome, starting with Newman, Frederick Faber and William Ward in 1845, and followed by Henry Manning and Robert Wilberforce a few years later. However, many of them did remain in the Church of England and led the Catholic revival therein. Keble and Pusey were among those who stayed.

During this period, Newman held the "branch" theory of the Catholic Church: Greek, Latin and Anglican:

> Each of these inherited the early undivided Church *in solido* as its own possession. Each branch was identical with that early undivided Church, and in the unity of that Church it had unity with the other branches.[3]

Newman also enthusiastically promoted the idea of the Anglican Church as the *Via Media* between Protestantism and Roman Catholicism. However, in the summer of 1839 he began to have doubts about the Anglican position. He was studying the Monophysite[4] controversy in the early centuries of the Church. As he worked on he became "seriously alarmed" because it seemed to him that the Christendom of the 16th and 19th centuries was reflected in the middle of the 5th century. Looking at that reflection he saw himself in the position of a Monophysite. It seemed to him that the *Via Media* of the day had been occupied by the Monophysites, while the more extreme position in the controversy taken by the Eutychians was the equivalent of the Protestant view. The Church of Rome occupied the same position in the 5th century as in the 16th and 19th centuries.

The question in Newman's mind now was: if the Eutychians and Monophysites were in fact heretics, were not the Protestants and Anglicans also heretics? He pointed out that it was generally considered that the English Church received the Council of Chalcedon, which took place in the 5th century. It was, he said, difficult to argue against the Fathers at the Tridentine Council without at the same time arguing against those at Chalcedon which had resolved the controversy of the day and declared the true belief of the Christian Church; it was difficult to condemn the Popes in the 16th century and not those in the 5th century.

With regard to Pope Leo, who had been Pope at the time of Chalcedon, Newman wrote:

> I found that *he* had made the Fathers of the Council unsay their decree and pass another, so that (humanly speaking) we owe it to Pope Leo at this day that the Catholic Church holds the true doctrine. I found that Pope Leo based his authority upon St Peter. I found the Fathers of the Council crying out "Peter hath spoken by the mouth of Leo", when they altered their decree.[5]

Newman was then shown a copy of Nicholas Wiseman's article *The Anglican Claims of Apostolic Succession*, published in the *Dublin Review*. In the article Wiseman[6] had used another controversy from ancient Church history — that of the Donatists[7] — to show that where schism was concerned in the early Church, it was a recognised principle and rule that those who had separated themselves from Rome were, by the fact of that separation, judged to be in schism. Wiseman argued that the Anglican Church was in schism, having separated itself

44

from the Church of Rome. In the article were the words of St Augustine of Hippo: *Securus judicat orbis terrarum* ("the whole world is a safe judge"). The words struck Newman with a force he had never experienced from words before. The theory of the *Via Media* was "absolutely pulverised" in his view by the thought that "the deliberate judgment, in which the whole Church at length rests and acquiesces, is an infallible prescription and a final sentence against such portions of it as protest and secede."[8]

The thought that Rome might be right after all was a thought that came, and went again. Nevertheless, Newman's openness in seeking the truth and willingness to follow where it might lead him can be seen in a letter he wrote in 1839 to someone who had been similarly disturbed about the Anglican position and was considering whether the correct course would be to become a Roman Catholic:

> I really believe I say truly that, did I see cause to suspect that the Roman Church was in the right, I would try not to be unfaithful to the light given to me. And if at any future time, I have any view opened to me, I will try not to turn from it, but will pursue it, wherever it may lead. I am not aware of having any hindrance, whether from fear of clamour, or regard for consistency, or even love of friends, which could keep me from joining the Church of Rome, were I persuaded I ought to do so. . .

Newman continued by saying that in the normal way a person should take two or three years in prayerful preparation before coming to a final decision of this kind because of the dangers of being unduly influenced by various factors other than divine truth. There was a need, too, to take advice from people whom one trusted.

> When one considers how very solemn a step it is to change our religion, what a responsibility we incur if wrong, what an obligation there is under ordinary circumstances to remain where God has placed us, it seems to me but reasonable to say that such a step should not be taken without the guidance of others, without a long season of deliberation, and serious exercises during it. It is surely a much less sin to *remain in*, than to *change to*, a wrong faith.[9]

After the *Via Media* theory regarding the Anglican Church had collapsed in Newman's view, he was left simply with his three long-held, basic beliefs in dogma, a sacramental system, and opposition to Rome. However, the first two of these he considered were, in fact, better secured in the Roman Church rather than in the Anglican. Therefore, he was left with just opposition to Rome, in support of Anglicanism:

> My main argument for the Anglican claims lay in the positive and special charges which I could bring against Rome. I had no positive Anglican theory. I was very nearly pure Protestant. Lutherans had a sort of theology, so had Calvinists; I had none.[10]

He still considered that opposition to Rome to be well founded and it remained strong at this stage. However, slowly but surely the opposition began to lessen:

> I had a great and growing dislike, after the summer of 1839, to speak against the Roman Church herself or her formal doctrines. I was very averse to speak against doctrines which might possibly turn out to be true, though at the time I had no reason for thinking they were; or against the Church which had preserved them. I began to have misgivings, that, strong as my own feelings had been against her, yet in some things which I had said, I had taken the statements of Anglican divines for granted without weighing them for myself.[11]

He had been convinced from around the time of his early conversion experience that the Pope was the Antichrist predicted in the Scriptures, but from around 1833 onwards, he had formed theories which had changed his views. For example, he considered that the prophecies referred to the spirit of pagan Rome, not to the Roman Church; and that the Church in Rome had been instrumental in averting from the pagan city the divine punishments due to it.

In 1841, Newman wrote what proved to be the final Tract — No. 90 — of the Oxford Movement. He was anxious to show the Catholicity of the Anglican Church; that it was indeed part of the one Catholic and Apostolic Church to which the Creed referred. The Tract caused a furore by claiming that the Church of England's Thirty-nine Articles did not in fact condemn true Catholic practices, but only the abuse of such practices.

As Newman saw it, if the Anglican Church was a branch of the one Catholic Church, which had been taught revealed truth by Christ and the Apostles, then it must profess what had been professed from the beginning by the Catholic Church. Therefore, it was the duty of Anglicans to interpret the Thirty-nine Articles in the *true* Catholic sense, the sense of the Church Fathers, because Christ would not allow any portion of the Catholic Church to commit itself to statements which could not be given a meaning compatible with the teaching of the one Catholic Church.

Newman was subjected at this time to much public misrepresentation and accused of deception. It takes little imagination to consider the pain that was caused to him as a man of sincerity and forthrightness, eager to pursue the truth wherever it led him.

In 1838 Newman's Bishop had written to him saying that some expressions in the Tracts might cause people to fall into error. Newman, who considered himself first and foremost "a clergyman under the Bishop of Oxford",[12] offered to withdraw the Tracts from circulation if the Bishop so wished. However, it was only when No. 90 appeared that the Bishop felt things had gone too far and asked Newman to stop the Tracts altogether. Newman decided that if the Bishop demanded that Tract 90 be suppressed, he would do so but would also resign his living. "I could not in conscience act otherwise,"[13] he said. But agreement was reached that Newman should publish a letter stating the Bishop's wish that the Tracts should cease, and his objections to No. 90 in particular.

Newman resigned from the leadership of the Oxford Movement, but remained as Vicar of St Mary's. He continued to feel a responsibility for those who had come into the Oxford Movement through him. At this stage he did not consider that he should join the Roman Catholic Church and he tried to dissuade others from doing so. The reasons he gave for not encouraging others to join Rome were that he himself felt he could not in conscience do so and therefore should not encourage others to do something he would not do; he considered that some were being carried along by excitement and he firmly favoured a careful, considered approach; he was conscious of his duties to his Bishop and to the Anglican Church; and in some cases, they were young people who had been placed in his charge by their parents or superiors. His attitude at this time shows particularly clearly his prudent and conscientious character.

Following his resignation as leader of the Oxford Movement, Newman spent much time translating the work of St Athanasius. This reinforced his earlier doubts regarding the position of the Anglican Church. Again he saw comparisons with the history of the Arian heresy:[14] the Protestants as the full Arians; the Anglicans as semi-Arians; and Rome in the same position as then. And Rome had been the one that held to the truth.

Two further events added weight to Newman's

doubts. One was the increasing number of Anglican bishops condemning Tract 90 which in Newman's views was tantamount to denying Anglican Catholicity, and the other was the establishment of the Jerusalem bishopric by Parliament which meant that Protestants could place themselves under an Anglican bishop without having to renounce their errors and without due regard to whether they had been baptised or confirmed. The Anglican Church was ". . . not only forbidding any sympathy or concurrence with the Church of Rome, but it actually was courting an intercommunion with Protestant Prussia and the heresy of the Orientals. The Anglican Church might have the apostolical succession, as had the Monophysites; but such acts as were in progress led me to the gravest suspicion, not that it would soon cease to be a Church, but that it had never been a Church all along."[15]

To his bishop he wrote:

> May I be allowed to say, that I augur nothing but evil if we in any respect prejudice our title to be a branch of the Apostolic Church? . . . Men who learn, whether by means of documents or measures, whether from the statements or the acts of persons in authority, that our communion is not a branch of the one Church, I foresee with much grief, will be tempted to look out for that Church elsewhere.[16]

In February 1842, Newman went to live at Littlemore, about two miles from Oxford. It was part of St Mary's parish and he had earlier built a church there. The move was one he had been hoping to make for some time. With several other people he lived a semi-monastic life in spartan surroundings. He had already done much pastoral work there and in 1840 had written to his sister that the children's singing was improving and he was teaching them new tunes, leading them with a violin he had found and strung.

A person who greatly influenced him at this time was Dr Russell, President of the Catholic college of Maynooth in Ireland. Newman wrote of him: "He was always gentle, mild, unobtrusive, uncontroversial. He let me alone. He also gave me one or two books."[17]

One of the books was *St Alphonsus Liguori's Sermons*. Newman had read extracts of the Saint's writings previously, and disliked the "Mariolotry" he found in them. They had, he said, prejudiced him as much as anything else against the Roman Catholic Church. However, he found nothing of the kind in this book of Sermons. He asked Dr Russell if anything had been left out, and was told that a particular passage on the Blessed Virgin had been omitted as it was not considered that the more extreme devotions were appreciated outside Italy. Newman was relieved to find that tastes varied in this matter. He described the more extreme manifestations of devotion to the Blessed Virgin as having been "my great *crux* as regards Catholicism."[18] Such manifestations had nothing in common with the warm, solidly based devotion to Mary which he embraced and promoted among others.

Dr Russell also sent Newman a selection of Roman Catholic books circulating in Rome and he was surprised to find how little there was to object to in them. If Newman still had some reservations about devotions to Mary and the Saints, he had no difficulties with the *Spiritual Exercises of St Ignatius* which dealt with the soul's direct relationship with God.

He had never lost that thought about there being just two "self-evident beings, myself and my Creator" which had made so deep an impression on him at the age of fifteen. His search for religious truth, intellectual as it was, was also an affair of the heart. It was first and foremost about his relationship with God. Where did God want him? What did God want him to be? As he continued to search for the answer at Littlemore his daily life included much prayer, meditation and fasting. Sometimes he suffered from tiredness and headaches but he was unrelenting in his determination to follow the "Kindly Light".

The subject of the development of doctrine in the Christian Church had long been a favourite with Newman but it was at the end of 1842 and in 1843 that he devoted his attention to the matter. In the last of his fifteen sermons preached before Oxford University, on the Feast of the Purification, 2 February 1843, he spoke of the Blessed Virgin as a model for the development of Christian doctrine:

> Thus St Mary is our pattern of Faith, both in the reception and in the study of Divine Truth. She does not think it enough to accept, she dwells

upon it; not enough to possess, she uses it; not enough to assent, she develops it; not enough to submit the Reason, she reasons upon it; not indeed reasoning first, and believing afterwards, with Zacharias, yet first believing without reasoning; next, from love and reverence, reasoning after believing.[19]

In the same month Newman formally withdrew "all the hard things which I had said against the Church of Rome."[20] In September 1843 he resigned as Vicar of St Mary's in view of his interpretation of the Thirty-nine Articles being incompatible with the view held by the Church of England bishops. He preached his farewell sermon, the *"Parting of Friends"*, at Littlemore, on 25 September. The children of Littlemore were there, wearing the new clothes given to them by Newman as his parting gift.

It was still to be two years before Newman finally took the step of being received into the Roman Catholic Church. Throughout this period he was acutely aware of the pain he was giving to other people who had looked to him for guidance in religious matters.

In a letter to Mrs William Froude on 5 April 1844, Newman wrote:

My confidence against the Church of Rome lay in two things, first my feeling that we had the Apostolic Succession — next my conviction that her peculiar doctrines were not held by the Fathers.

As to the first of these, I acknowledged great irregularity in the transmission, and vast and various disorders and faults in our Church. But I got over all by the parallel of the Jewish Church which was a Church when Christ came, in spite of anomalies as great as ours. . . As to the second it was to me as clear as day (as it is now) that the honours paid in the Church of Rome to St Mary were not primitive.[21]

He had become unsettled on the first point by his reading of early Church history, the controversies therein, and the parallels he could see with the Reformation period and the 19th century. Along with this he came to regard the Anglican views about the oneness of the Church to be untenable. In another letter to Mrs Froude, dated 19 May 1844, he set out the difficulties: In what way did the Anglicans consider the Catholic Church to be one? he asked. His answer was:

They consider it a *succession*, propagated through different countries, independent in each country and claiming adherence of Christians in this or that country to itself as it exists in this or that country.

But, said Newman, when a person was baptised they were not baptised into a local church but into the Catholic Church which was spread throughout the world.

It puzzled me to make out, in what sense, on the hypothesis that Rome and England formed one Church, a man changed his Church who went from the English to the Roman branch, any more than he changed it, if he communicated here with the Church of Oxford, there with the Church of London. He changed his *faith* indeed; that is another matter; but how was he guilty of schism, how could he *change* his Church, when there was no *other* Church to change to?

Anglicans, he said, were forced to argue that there is only one bishop and church in each place and in England that was the Anglican Church and therefore the Roman Church was an intruder. That, he said, ignored the fact that the differences between the Anglican and Roman Church were concerned with doctrine and practice. He agreed with those who thought it absurd that a person who believed certain doctrines on the continent should be expected to change to different beliefs and practices on coming to England, if the Anglican and Roman Churches were each part of the one Catholic Church. Similarly, if the Anglican and Roman Churches were one, an Anglican ought to feel free to communicate in areas where the Roman Church had succession, but this was not the case. Having looked at the Anglican theory of local Episcopacy which gave rise to "these absurdities", Newman said he found it "as untenable as its consequences".[22]

Two months later, he wrote about the idea of the development of doctrine:

> I am far more certain (according to the Fathers) that we *are* in a state of culpable separation *than* that developments do *not* exist under the gospel, and that the Roman developments are *not* true ones.
>
> I am far more certain that *our* (modern) doctrines are wrong, *than* that the Roman (modern) doctrines are wrong.
>
> Granting that the Roman (special) doctrines are

not found drawn out in the early Church, yet I think there is sufficient trace of them in it, to recommend and prove them, *on the hypothesis* of the Church having a divine guidance, though not sufficient to prove them by itself. So that the question simply turns on the nature of the promise of the Spirit made to the Church.

The proof of the *Roman* (special) doctrines is as strong (or stronger) in Antiquity, as that of certain doctrines which *both we and the Romans* hold. . .

The analogy of the Old Testament and the New leads to the acknowledgement of doctrinal developments. . .[23]

To bring his own final misgivings about leaving the Anglican Church for Rome to an end, he decided to write an essay on the development of doctrine. If, when he had finished that work, his convictions regarding Rome were not weaker, he would ask to be received into that Church. From the beginning of 1845 to the autumn, Newman worked at this project and came to see:

The principle of development not only accounted for certain facts, but was in itself a remarkable philosophical phenomenon, giving a character to the whole course of Christian thought.[24]

Newman was finally convinced, even before he had fully completed the manuscript, that the correct step for him now was to move to Rome.

Notes

[1] *Apologia*, p. 63.

[2] Cf ibid., pp. 67–70.

[3] Ibid., p. 84.

[4] Monophysites believed that Christ had only one nature, a divine nature, his humanity having been absorbed by his divinity. The Council of Chalcedon (451 AD) condemned this heresy and affirmed that Christ was both fully human and fully divine, possessing two distinct natures, human and divine, "without confusion, without change, without division, without separation." Eutyches (c. 378–454 AD) is regarded as the founder of Monophysitism.

[5] Letter to Mrs William Froude, 5/4/1844. *Letters*, edited by Stanford and Spark, p. 100.

[6] Nicholas Wiseman (1802–1865). He was Rector of the English College in Rome, from 1828–1840. He then became firstly Coadjutor to the Vicar Apostolic of the Midland District in England, and then Pro-Vicar Apostolic in London, before being appointed the first Archbishop of Westminster when the Roman Catholic hierarchy was restored in England and Wales in 1850.

[7] Donatists held that the validity of the sacraments was dependant on the spiritual state of the person administering them.

[8] *Apologia*, p. 121.

[9] Letter to R. Williams (not sent) 10/11/1839. *CP* Vol. III, pp. 1001–1003.

[10] *Apologia*, p. 123.

[11] Ibid., p. 126.

[12] Letter to E. B. Pusey, 26/8/1838. *LD* VI, p. 308.

[13] *Apologia*, p. 193.

[14] Arians denied the true Divinity of Christ, regarding him as neither co-eternal nor co-equal with the Father. The heresy was condemned by the Council of Nicea in 325 AD.

[15] *Apologia*, p. 143.

[16] Ibid., p. 144.

[17] Ibid., p. 183.

[18] Ibid., p. 183.

[19] *University Sermons*, No. XV, p. 313.

[20] *Apologia*, p. 187.

[21] *Letters*, edited by Stanford and Spark, pp. 99–100.

Mrs Froude was the sister-in-law of Hurrell Froude and James Anthony Froude, the historian. She became a Roman Catholic some ten years after Newman. Her husband was a railway engineer and a naval architect.

22 Ibid., pp. 107–108.
23 Ibid., p. 118.
24 *Apologia*, p. 185.

4

"One step enough for me"

One of the things that had troubled Newman was a lack of the example of holiness in the Roman Catholic Church of that time. And holiness was a mark of the true Church of Christ. The example was provided for Newman by an Italian Passionist priest, Fr Dominic Barberi. He had come to England after many years of waiting, and praying for the land he had not seen but had been given to understand in prayer would be a place for which he had a special mission. He had acted in the very way that Newman had exclaimed in a letter in 1841 should be followed by Roman Catholic missionaries if they wished to convert England: "Let them go barefooted into our manufacturing towns, let them preach to the people, like St Francis Xavier, let them be pelted and trampled on, and I will own that they can do what we cannot."[1]

Unbeknown to Newman, Fr Dominic was going around poorly dressed, preaching and frequently having things thrown at him. Newman said of him:

His very look had about it something holy. When his form came within sight, I was moved to the depths in the strangest way. The gaiety and affability of his manner in the midst of all his sanctity was itself a holy sermon. No wonder then that I became his convert and his penitent.[2]

On 3 October 1845, Newman sent in his resignation as a Fellow of Oriel. In a letter written on the same day, he mentioned that Fr Dominic was coming there on his way to Belgium, by accident. The next day, in another letter, he said that Fr Dominic was coming and it was likely that he would admit him to the Roman Catholic Church. On the 8th he wrote a number of letters to be sent out after his reception had taken place. Fr Dominic arrived that night, to be greeted with the news that John Henry Newman wished to be received into the Roman Catholic Church. Soaked by the rain during a five-hour journey on top of a coach, Fr Dominic could only exclaim with all his heart: "God be praised".

Fr Dominic's vivid description of the scene had been related time and again:

> I took up my position by the fire to dry myself. The door opened, and what a spectacle it was for me to see at my feet John Henry Newman begging me to hear his confession and admit him into the bosom of the Catholic Church! And there by the fire he began his general confession with extraordinary humility and devotion.[3]

It was eleven o'clock at night and so the confession was resumed and completed the following day. In the evening, Newman and two others from the Littlemore group, Richard Stanton and Frederick Bowles,[4] made their profession of faith as Roman Catholics. Fr Dominic came away with the belief that Newman was "one of the most humble and lovable men I have met in my life."[5]

Fr Dominic was beatified by Pope Paul VI in 1963. His simplicity has often been mentioned but the idea of a "simple priest" should not be overdone, as a kind of foil to Newman's genius. Fr Dominic was not only a mystic of great holiness; he was also a person of considerable intellectual ability as can be seen in the fact that before he came to England he had written a seven-volume manual of moral theology and a six-volume manual of philosophy. A full catalogue of his literary output takes up some fifteen pages. He had occupied a number of important posts in the Passionist Congregation in Italy, including that of Provincial. And now he had been sent to establish the Passionist Congregation in England. Newman and Dominic were each quick to recognise the holiness of the other — an example of saintly heart speaking to saintly heart. Newman accurately assessed him as "a shrewd, clever man, but as unaffected and simple as a child, and most singularly kind in his thoughts of religious persons in our communion . . . I wish all persons were as charitable as I know him to be."[6]

Cardinal Wiseman described Dominic as "a

lion in the might of his intelligence and a child in the simplicity of his heart.''[7]

For Newman the journey was in one sense over, in another sense only just beginning. Fr Dominic had warned Newman and his companions that they were but babes in the faith. What the future might hold, Newman did not know. He did not ask to see the distant scene —'one step enough for me'.

Shortly after becoming a Roman Catholic, Newman set out to get to know English Catholics in various parts of the country. Among the places he visited was Oscott College, Birmingham, where he was confirmed on 1 November 1845. He was anxious not only to learn about Catholics and Roman Catholicism in practice, but also to remove any prejudice or suspicions that might remain about him and his conversion.

Newman moved from his beloved Littlemore on 22 February 1846. Before leaving the house he kissed the mantelpiece and his bed, so dear had the place been to him. He was not only leaving Littlemore, he was also leaving Oxford after some thirty years there, and would not visit it again for thirty-two years. The new home for himself and his companions from Littlemore was at Maryvale, the old Oscott College which was given to them for their use and which Newman renamed in honour of the Blessed Virgin; his dislike of certain expressions of devotion to her in no way lessened his deep devotion to her.

In March 1846, a visitor to Maryvale, Robert

Coffin, wrote that, despite the house being only half furnished and their books not yet being arranged, ". . . all seemed very happy and well satisfied . . . especially Newman, who was much more so than I had expected to see him after his sore trial in leaving poor old Littlemore: as usual he is the life of the whole party and keeps all cheerful and in good humour."[8]

Newman gave as much care and thought to discerning the Will of God for himself in the Roman Catholic Church as he had over deciding whether God was leading him into it in the first place. Prayer and taking the advice of others figured largely in the process of discernment.

He had some thoughts about starting a Congregation of the Most Holy Trinity. The title and object of the proposed Congregation reflected Newman's own great love for the Trinity. His humility, derived from an awareness of the infinite greatness and mystery of God and of human nothingness, can be seen in his ideas for such a Congregation. Faced with the rationalism of the times, he stressed the need for its members to teach and preach in every way about the mysteries of the faith, and to lovingly adore the Trinity, the Incarnation and the Eucharist *as* mysteries. A deep sense of their own nothingness as human beings was also to be nourished.

The Co-adjutor to the Vicar Apostolic in the Midland District of England, Dr Wiseman considered that Newman and his companions should join the Oratorian congregation. However, while Newman certainly welcomed the idea of being under the patronage of

St Philip Neri, who established the Oratorians in Rome, he felt some uncertainty about that being the correct path for them to follow because the Oratorians lived and worked in towns and cities whereas Maryvale, where he and his companions were living, was out in the country. Keeping an open mind, Newman continued the diligent search.

He was drawn to the Vincentians, but he also felt that the need in England was for Dominicans, the Order of Preachers, "persons who will oppose heresy whether by writing, preaching or teaching." But he had some reservations as to whether they had preserved the traditions of their Order and whether their mendicant nature was really suited to the times. Pondering the various possibilities, Newman concluded: "But I shall do just what they tell me to do in Rome."[9]

On 7 September 1846 Newman, together with Ambrose St John,[10] set out on the journey to Rome. On the way, Newman continued to further his knowledge about various Orders, visiting the Generalate of the Vincentians in Paris, and the Jesuit House in the Rue des Postes. They arrived in Rome on 28 October having stayed for a month in Milan to study Italian.

Newman and St John began their theological studies as planned in Rome, while still examining various Rules and the life and work of several Orders. Finally, after much prayer and discussion, Newman concluded that the Oratorian way of life was the one best suited to their group. He later noted the main reasons for the choice: "Whereas the tastes of all of us were very different, the Oratory allowed greater scope for them than any other Institution; again it seemed more adapted than any other for Oxford and Cambridge men."[11] The choice made, Newman wrote to Wiseman, and made a Novena visiting the tomb of St Peter each day. Wiseman's reply was one of full approval. In the meantime, the Pope had enthusiastically welcomed the idea of Newman establishing the Oratory in England and suggested that his companions at Maryvale should be asked to come out to Rome to undergo a novitiate with Newman.

From Rome Newman wrote to Henry Wilberforce: "I was happy at Oriel, happier at Littlemore, as happy or happier still at Maryvale — and happiest here."[12]

Against this one has to balance his comments regarding that time, written later in his journal. There he writes:

> How dreary my first year at Maryvale, when I was the gaze of so many eyes at Oscott, as if some wild incomprehensible beast, caught by the hunter, and a spectacle for Dr Wiseman to exhibit to strangers, as himself being the hunter who captured it. I did not realise this at the time except in its discomfort. . .[13]

The resolution of the two very different views is perhaps to be found in the last sentence: "I did not realise this at the time except in its discomfort." At the time he felt discomfort at being an object of curiosity but "dreariness" may have been far more apparent to him at the time he was writing this which was, in fact, in 1863, some eighteen years after the event and at a time when he was feeling understandably depressed and frustrated regarding his life in the Catholic Church. The same resolution can be applied to the remainder of his journal covering this period but written long afterwards.

During his time in Rome, he encountered some queries about his work on the development of doctrine, and on faith and reason. His attitude, as he took steps to clarify what he had said, was expressed in a letter:

> I am not maintaining what I say is all true, but I wish to *assist in investigating* and bringing to light *great principles* necessary for the day — and the only way to bring them out is *freely* to investigate, with the inward habitual intention, which I trust I have, always to be submitting what I say to the judgement of the Church.[14]

Newman and Ambrose St John attended lectures in dogmatic and moral theology each day. The standard was hardly taxing for Newman, being aimed at "beginners", and St John teasingly accused him of nodding off during some of the lectures.

Newman was ordained a priest on 30 May 1847 at the Propaganda College and a month later, with his companions, began the Oratorian novitiate in the monastery attached to the Basilica of Santa Croce in Rome. In Newman's view the Christian love and an unvowed obedience required of the Oratorians resembled early Christianity. The main mortification for the Oratorian came naturally from living in a community; for the community to be united there was a vital need for the members to adjust their minds, wills, opinions and conduct. Newman's short rule of perfection given to the Oratorians can equally be applied to everyone else: "He then is perfect who does the work of the day perfectly, and we need not go beyond this to seek for perfection."[15]

An openness of spirit characterised Newman in his embracing of the Oratorian way of life. Having studied its history and its spirit he could grasp what were the essential elements of being an Oratorian and of its particular apostolate in the Church. He held on to these but set about making necessary adaptations to suit it for establishment in England. In the course of this adaptation he was particularly concerned to understand and return to the original spirit of St Philip Neri, a concern which was the hallmark of renewal in the religious life after Vatican II. Newman's love for truth can be seen in the diligence he showed in learning about the Oratorian spirit and life and in a faithful adaptation of it for different circumstances and surroundings. He had a great love for St Philip which was expressed in his constant endeavouring to be faithful to his spirit and in imitating his virtues, and he had immense confidence in his intercession. His attitude towards the Saint was always one of gratitude.

In a sermon on the mission of St Philip, Newman spoke of what the Saint had drawn from three other great saints: Benedict,

Dominic and Ignatius of Loyola. From Benedict, Philip had learned what to *be*; Dominic's example had shown him what to *do*; and from Ignatius he learnt *how* to do it. St Philip had particularly loved the writings of St Paul, Apostle of the Gentiles, and Newman considered that it was to St Paul one must look to see the success of St Philip's techniques and influence. Like St Paul, St Philip had made himself "all things to all men".

In looking at the things enjoined by Newman on his fellow Oratorians it is possible to see his own attitudes and actions reflected: the imperfections and mistakes of others should be hidden, as far as was right — they should not be drawn into open view; love and trust should abound in the Oratory with each person considering the others as their kindest friends.

Newman saw the work of the Oratory as being to form good secular priests. Its special apostolate was in fact "any work suitable to the priesthood". He considered that the priestly work most typical of St Philip's spirit was preaching, prayer and administering the sacraments, especially Confession.

Newman returned home from Rome to England via Loreto, a shrine he particularly loved because of its connection with the mystery of the Incarnation.

He set up the Oratory at Maryvale on 1 February 1848. Two weeks later Frederick Faber[16] and the group of young converts he had gathered into a community known as the 'Wilfridians' were admitted by Newman as

Oratorians. This was at the request of Faber and of Dr Nicholas Wiseman who was now Pro-Vicar Apostolic of the London District; the Hierarchy of England and Wales and the dioceses were not restored until 1850.

Problems were not slow in coming. Faber had, as it were, thrown himself at the feet of Newman asking him to treat him as a "corpse", such was his willingness to obey Newman. However, on a more practical level, Faber omitted to tell Newman that St Wilfrid's, formerly Cotton Hall, at Cheadle in Staffordshire, which was the base used by Faber and his group of 'Wilfridians', supplied the missions in the area and was a binding commitment he could not relinquish. It was left to Newman to discover what was involved, in a long correspondence with the Earl of Shrewsbury. The financial consequences of this encumbrance with which Newman was landed were that Maryvale had to be given up and St Wilfrid's used as the Oratory. The move there was completed in October 1848. In the same month, Newman had begun also to set up an Oratory in Alcester Street, Birmingham, to meet the requirements of the Papal Brief. The Alcester Street Oratory officially opened on 2 February 1849.

Shortly afterwards the Oratory was established in London in King William Street, and Newman appointed Faber as the Rector there. Newman remained in Birmingham but was present for the opening of the London church on 31 May 1849.

Birmingham at the time had few Catholics among its 600,000 population. Those few were for the most part poor and uneducated: immigrants from Ireland. Newman and his companions, in fact, had chosen to set up their Oratory in an area which made it possible to serve the poor, following St Philip's precept of loving to be unknown. Newman was often seen hurrying along taking bottles of medicine to the sick among the poor in the area. He himself knew considerable poverty at this time. He had to write to Faber on one occasion: "Literally I am penniless. . ."

After only a few months at Alcester Street, Newman was asked by Bishop Ullathorne if two of the Oratorians could be spared to go and assist the two priests in Bilston, who were overwhelmed with work due to a cholera epidemic. Typically, Newman went himself, with Ambrose St John. They found the epidemic all but over and only needed to stay for two days but their willingness to go there and the promptness with which they had carried out the Bishop's request were remembered by him long afterwards in an appreciative letter he wrote to Newman in 1864 following an address given to Newman by the priests of the diocese after the publication of the *Apologia Pro Vita Sua*.

Newman was remembered affectionately by the boys in Alcester Street. They later spoke of his kindness and the easy manner he had had with them and of the respect they quickly gained for him. Newman was particularly liked by young people. They felt at ease with him. And his treatment of them shows very much the human face of Newman.

Newman's *Discourses to Mixed Congregations* came from his early months at Alcester Street. His sermons had been directed to both Catholics and non-Catholics, and he decided to publish them as a book.

From May to July 1850, Newman gave a series of lectures in London which were also later published as a book: *Lectures on Certain Difficulties felt by Anglicans in Catholic Teaching*. The lectures not only brought about a number of conversions, and increased his correspondence from people seeking advice and spiritual help, they also made a highly favourable impression in Rome. In August he was given an Honorary Doctorate of Divinity.

In the same month, the London Oratory became an independent house. Faber was elected Superior. He immediately wrote to Newman stating a whole list of powers he thought Newman should have relating to the London Oratory, as its founder. Newman, on the other hand, produced a paper on the matter with far fewer powers than Faber had suggested.

On 29 September 1850 came the restoration of the Roman Catholic Hierarchy in England and Wales. There was much public concern over "Papal aggression". In an attempt to set about destroying the prejudice that was still evident against Roman Catholics, Newman gave a series of lectures, later published as *Lectures on the Present Position of Catholics in England*. He used humour and irony to show the absurdity of

71

the prejudice, and appealed in the final lecture for a Catholic laity who would have sufficient knowledge of their Faith to be able to explain their beliefs whenever necessary:

> . . . I want a laity, not arrogant, not rash in speech, not disputations, but men who know their religion, who enter into it, who know just where they stand, who know what they hold, and what they do not, who know their creed so well, that they can give an account of it, who know so much of history that they can defend it. . . I wish you to enlarge your knowledge, to cultivate your reason, to get an insight into the relation of truth to truth, to learn to view things as they are, to understand how faith and reason stand to each other. . .[17]

At this time, a former Dominican Friar from Italy was giving talks in England about the inquisition and its horrors from which he had suffered. His audience were unaware of the fact that he was known in Italy to have committed many immoralities in Italy and Malta. Witnesses were not lacking.

After much prayer and thought, and consulting two lawyers regarding possible libel action, Newman decided he should speak out and tell the sordid truth about the man, Dr Giacinto Achilli, to prevent him doing further harm to the reputation of the Roman Catholic Church. With the Evangelical Alliance behind him, Achilli promptly sued Newman for libel. Slowness on the part of Wiseman in London and the Bishops' representative in Rome, Monsignor George Talbot, in obtaining the necessary evidence against Achlli meant that the case was sent to trial, and Newman faced the very real prospect of going to prison.

It was now necessary not only to find witnesses but also to persuade them to travel to England to be heard, and not to disappear again when the trial was postponed from February to June 1852. Newman suffered much from the suspense but continued to trust in Divine Providence:

> I have not had an interruption to the simple feeling that I am in God's hands, who knows what He is about, and that everything will be well, and that I shall be borne thro' everything — I cannot at all divine the event, but that it will be good in some way or another, I am *sure*.[18]

The trial ended with Judge and jury finding that Newman had not proved his allegations against Achilli and he was therefore found guilty of libel on 24 June 1852. The evidence given in court had in fact given the moral victory to Newman, and the *Times* newspaper considered that justice had *not* been done as far as Newman was concerned. However, the court's verdict meant that Newman had a further agonising wait to find out his sentence. His lawyers' attempts to get a retrial were rejected and on 31 January 1853 Newman was fined £100 with imprisonment until it was paid. Fortunately, a fund set up to pay the fine, and the costs which amounted to around £10,000, was well supported by people from many parts of the world.

Throughout the months awaiting trial and

then the sentence, Newman had put his trust completely in prayer. He considered that prayers to St Anthony of Padua, the finder of things that have been lost, had been the reason for success in finding the necessary witnesses in Italy and persuading them to come to England.

The whole affair was yet another example of Newman's concern for truth, and his willingness to suffer in its cause.

During the period of the Achilli trial, Newman was also involved in building a new Oratory at Edgbaston. He and his companions moved in on 2 February 1852, but they still looked after the chapel in Alcester Street. By this time the Oratory was stretched to the limits with its varied apostolic works including the workhouse chaplaincy which was undertaken from 1852. Something like 600 Catholics passed through the workhouse in the course of a year, and about 150 were there at any one time.

On 13 July 1852, in the midst of his many worries and activities, Newman gave his famous "Second Spring" sermon at the first synod of the new Westminster Province, held at Oscott. Although the sermon was related to the re-establishment of the Roman Catholic hierarchy in England and Wales, it is one that can be relished by all Christians who value their common heritage, who lament the pain they have inflicted on each other, while praising the heroism of those prepared to suffer and die rather than deny their faith, and who hope to be united through the grace of God.

Notes

1. Letter to J. R. Bloxham, 23/2/1841. *CP* Vol. III, pp. 1038–1039.
2. Urban Young, *The Life and Letters of Ven. Dominic (Barberi) CP*, Burns Oates and Washbourne, London, 1926, p. 261.
3. *Newman's Journey*, p. 114.
4. Frederick Bowles and Richard Stanton went on to join the Oratorians with Newman. Frederick Bowles remained with the Birmingham Oratory; Richard Stanton became Secretary of the London Oratory.
5. *CP* Vol. XIV, p. 4999. See also: *Newman's Journey*, p. 115.
6. *CP* Vol. II, p. 632. See also: Alfred Wilson, *Blessed Dominic Barberi*, p. 304.
7. Alfred Wilson, *Blessed Dominic Barberi*, CTS, p. 14. And *Testimonies to Blessed Dominic, Passionist*, p. 2, Passionists of St Joseph's Province, England, 1982.
8. *CP* Vol. IV, p. 1294. Robert Coffin, Vicar of St Mary Magdalene's, in Oxford, before his conversion to Roman Catholicism, later joined the Oratorians and was Rector at St Wilfrid's. However, he eventually left and joined the Redemptorists.
9. Letter to T. F. Knox, 20/8/1846. *LD* XI, p. 227.
10. Ambrose St John joined the Littlemore community in 1843, and was received into the Roman Catholic Church on 2 October 1845. He became Newman's closest friend. Newman, at his own request, was buried in the same grave as St John.
11. *CP* Vol. IV, p. 1301.
12. Letter to H. Wilberforce, 13/12/1846. *LD* XI, p. 294. Henry Wilberforce was the son of William Wilberforce who was famous for his work towards the abolition of the slave trade and of slavery in general throughout the British Empire.
13. *Autobiographical Writings*, p. 255.
14. Letter to J. D. Dalgairns, 8/2/1847. *LD* XII, p. 29.
15. *CP* Vol. VIII, p. 2973.
16. Frederick William Faber (1814–1863). He became a Roman Catholic in 1845, and is best remembered now as the writer of many well-loved hymns and devotional books.
17. *Lectures on the Present Position of Catholics in England*, p. 390.
18. Letter to R. Stanton, 4/12/1851. *CP* Vol. VIII, p. 2643.

5

Beset with problems

In 1851 Archbishop Cullen of Armagh had asked Newman to become the first Rector of the proposed Catholic University in Ireland. Newman agreed and he was working on his *Discourses on the Scope and Nature of University Education* while awaiting trial in the Achilli affair. It has been said that "modern thinking on university education is a series of footnotes to Newman's lectures and essays."[1]

As with other projects which Newman was called upon to undertake, this one was beset with problems. The founding of the University was not helped by the fact that the Irish bishops were divided regarding the feasibility of the project and there was delay in opening it.

Newman was called upon to go to Dublin in October 1853 to begin work as Rector. In view of the difficulties arising from mixed views on the project among the Irish bishops, clergy and lay people, he asked for some kind of official recognition that would publicly show what his position was and what authority he had. The reply came from Dr Cullen, who had become Archbishop of Dublin in 1852, that it was not yet possible to make anything public. Newman wrote explaining the problem to Dr Wiseman.

The latter had already asked the Pope for a Brief approving both the University and Newman's appointment as its Rector. Wiseman had also suggested that Newman be made a bishop, an idea which Newman at first opposed but then relented, seeing that it would be useful in his dealings with the bishops and clergy. The Pope had warmly approved the idea and Newman's own bishop, Dr Ullathorne, also enthusiastically welcomed the idea. However, Dr Cullen subsequently successfully blocked any such move. Newman was given no reason and he asked for none.

In recent years, letters found in the archives of the Propaganda in Rome show that Dr Cullen wrote three letters in the early part of 1854 saying that he had heard of the proposal to make Newman a bishop and, although he welcomed the idea, he considered that this should be delayed until the University's affairs were more in order. He spoke of Newman being impractical whereas, in fact, Newman was highly organised and efficient.

Newman was left in the embarrassing position of having been told unofficially by Wiseman and Ullathorne that he was to be made a bishop, and having even received gifts for the occasion of his episcopal consecration from people who had also learnt of the proposed move, only for the matter to be dropped with no explanation. Notwithstanding this poor, to put it mildly, treatment, Newman pressed on with his work of setting up the University. In this he was still working very much as a champion of truth. As Rector of the

University he saw himself continuing the battle he had been fighting at Oxford against "liberalism" (indifferentism) in religious matters, and producing an educated Catholic laity who, in turn, could defend the truth of their Faith and play a leading part in society in general. To him the advantages of higher education could be summed up in the phrase the "cultivation of the intellect".

The Papal Brief for the University came in April 1854, with no mention now of Newman being made a bishop, and the bishops met in May and gave their approval to Newman as Rector and gave him temporary power to designate professors and other university officials. The power of final appointment was to remain with the bishops. After some problems relating to the appointments of professors and lecturers, the University officially opened on 3 November 1854.

During his time as Rector of the University in Dublin, Newman was also still Superior of the Birmingham Oratory. He was greatly disturbed to find in October 1855 that, three months previously, the Oratorians in London had applied to Rome for a dispensation from the Rule that forbade Oratorians to direct nuns or hear their confessions as it took them away from their special apostolate. The request to Rome had been put forward in such a way as to make it sound as though it was also coming from the Birmingham Oratory. This was not, of course, the case and Newman along with the Oratorians in Birmingham were much alarmed that such a misconception should have arisen because it affected a strong matter of principle and could have major implications for the future.

Each Oratory is independent of any other and cannot arbitrarily act in such a way as will affect other houses. Unlike religious orders and congregations in general, the Oratorians do not take vows; their lives are directed by the Oratorian Rule. While a particular house might seek a dispensation from one of the rules because of particular circumstances, they have no right to involve other houses. If this were to happen the stability of the Oratorian way of life would be severely threatened.

Newman, as the one who had established the Oratory in England, felt duty bound to oppose what the London Oratory had done. He wrote to Faber, who was the Superior in London, on 8 November 1855, and pointed out that what had been done had, albeit unintentionally, involved Birmingham. He asked Faber to write to the Propaganda in Rome and ask them for some formal acknowledgement recognising the independence of individual Oratorian houses. Faber and the London Oratorians refused Newman's request. Newman consulted with his fellow Oratorians in Birmingham and wrote once again, with the same negative result. Matters became more serious because the Secretary of the London Oratory wrote to Newman saying that they had not asked for a dispensation from the Rule — only for an interpretation of it. This was worse because an official interpretation would automatically have affected all the other houses whereas a dispensation was limited. Again, it was the implications for the future which were of primary concern to Newman. In a letter to Wiseman dated 19 October 1855 expressing concern, Newman pointed out that, in fact, there had been no need to involve Rome in the first place regarding any interpretation as there was provision in the Rule itself for explaining any portion of it.

In the end Newman went to Rome himself, visiting various Oratories in Italy on the way, and enquiring about the interpretation of the Rule. In Rome, he set about pressing for a ruling that each Oratory was independent and that the Holy See should do nothing which would lead to the action of one house affecting another. All was well and the dispensation was given to the London house only, and for a period of three years. It had been assumed in Rome that the original request would not have been made without Newman having been told about it.

No sooner had the London Oratorians heard that Newman had gone to Rome to sort out the matter than they wrote to Rome expressing the sincere hope that nothing would be done without their being consulted. They feared that Newman was trying to gain some kind of official jurisdiction over them, a kind of generalate. They also wrote to the various Italian Oratories voicing the same concern regarding a generalate. They need not have worried. Replies showed that Newman was not in any way speaking against the London Oratory but was simply putting various questions to gather information. One reply spoke of Newman showing such humility and gentleness that he had left them greatly edified.

Problems and misunderstandings continued to arise between Birmingham and London. Faber despatched two priests to Rome to obtain a separate Brief for the London Oratory which would prevent the setting up of another Oratory in London, which Newman had it in mind to do. He considered there would be less risk of problems arising over the Rule in future if there were more than just two Oratories in England.

Newman has been accused of being ultrasensitive in the sense of being touchy and easily hurt. It was, in fact, the London Oratorians who tried to reduce the issue to one of no more than wounded feelings on the part of Newman without seeming able to appreciate the potential damage of their actions to the Oratorian way of life in England. Newman was extremely conscious of the duties and obligations he had of establishing the Oratory in England on a firm and wholly accurate footing in keeping with the spirit of St Philip Neri. When the Birmingham Oratorians sent a statement to London giving their view of all that had happened between the two Oratories, London simply broke off all relations with Birmingham. Newman forbade his own community in Birmingham to speak about the differences that had arisen between the two Oratories so as not to damage Faber's reputation. They were silent. Not so the London Oratorians who damaged Newman's reputation with their gossip.

Newman's problems in Dublin were not diminishing. In February 1856 he returned there from Rome to find that although the University was making progress, the Irish bishops were keeping it at arm's length because they considered that Archbishop Cullen was exercising too great a control over it. The Archbishop gave rise to difficulties by refusing to make necessary decisions and by not setting up a finance committee of lay people as requested by Newman and the other bishops. Newman himself funded the University church.

Newman decided to resign as Rector in 1857, keeping to his initial intention of remaining in that position for three years. In all he had made well over fifty crossings between England and Ireland; the many heavy commitments were taking their toll on his health, and he was needed at the Oratory. All who were involved in the University were deeply reluctant to accept his resignation. Archbishop Cullen put forward the idea of appointing a resident Vice-Rector to relieve Newman of the need to be resident in Dublin, but it soon became clear that Cullen still wanted Newman to be resident for longer than Newman and the Oratorians wished. Newman considered that a layman should be appointed Vice-Rector, with preference being given to someone already familiar with the workings of the University. Newman insisted that it would have to be someone he could trust.

The bishops' preference was for a priest to be appointed, and Newman was not, in fact, consulted about the appointment. He waited for a further year for the appointment of a Vice-Rector, refusing to accept a salary after February 1858, before finally resigning in November. He dealt with all the University matters during this time, in Birmingham.

In August 1857, Cardinal Wiseman had asked, on behalf of the bishops of England and Wales, if Newman would undertake a new, English translation of the Bible. Newman did not feel particularly suited to the task and in order to undertake it had to set aside two other projects he had in mind, but he considered that the request of the bishops should take priority. He duly obtained necessary materials and approached a number of people to assist in the task. In September he wrote to Wiseman to ask how expenses were going to be met. One year later the reply came that the copyright would be reserved to Newman. In other words, no money for expenses already incurred or to be incurred before actual publication was to be forthcoming. When the American bishops approached him to know if they could make it a joint translation, Newman had to reply that he was still waiting for instructions from the hierarchy in England and Wales. In fact, Newman heard no more about the project; it was simply dropped.

In 1859 Newman was asked by the bishops to take on the editorship of the journal, *The Rambler*. It had been critical of the bishops and they considered that without a change of editor and editorial spirit the journal would have to be censured by them in their pastoral letters. Newman was regarded as someone who was acceptable to both the hierarchy and to those who had been running and supporting *The Rambler*. It was an extremely hot seat, but Newman accepted it as that was what the bishops wished. Bishop Ullathorne wrote to thank him for taking on the task. However, Newman was soon in hot water for suggesting that if the laity had been consulted prior to the definition of the dogma of the Immaculate Conception, it was even more appropriate that they should be consulted with regard to such matters as education which so closely concerned them.

Bishop Ullathorne suggested to Newman that he should resign after the July issue. Newman did so but in that issue he defended his remarks about the laity, in an article, *On Consulting the Faithful in Matters of Doctrine*. He carefully defined what he meant by "consulting" in these matters and what he did not mean. He had used the word in the sense of enquiring into or looking at what the faithful believed or thought; not in the sense of asking their advice or taking their counsel. They were to be regarded as giving testimony or witness to revealed doctrine by their beliefs. There had been periods in the Church's history when the faith was preserved, not by the Pope or Bishops of the day but by the body of the faithful, the *consensus fidelium*. Newman pointed to this being the case, for example, during the time of the Arian controversy. With regard to defining dogma, the universal mind of the Church could be discovered by looking at what the faithful did, in fact, believe. Such definitions are not new truths plucked out of the air; they are expressions of existing belief within the Church. When there was a consensus of belief throughout the Church, that was the infallible voice of the Church.

Newman's explanation of what he meant by "consulting" resulted in his being delated to Rome for heresy by Bishop Brown of Newport whose inaccurate Latin translation gave an heretical sense. When he heard of this delation, Newman wrote to Cardinal Wiseman to ask which parts of the article had given rise to such action, and said he would be only too willing to explain them further. In April 1860, the future Cardinal Manning wrote on behalf of Cardinal Wiseman to say that the latter hoped to bring the matter to an acceptable end. Newman heard no more. He did not know that Wiseman had received questions from the Propaganda Congregation in Rome for which it asked him to obtain answers from Newman. Wiseman failed to pass the questions to Newman and the result was that for seven years Newman was under a cloud in Rome, it being thought he had simply refused to answer the questions. During that period Cardinal Barnabò, Prefect of the Propaganda Congregation, had written to Bishop Ullathorne to complain that no word had been received from Newman but Ullathorne who was, in fact, well disposed towards Newman, said the matter had been placed in Cardinal Wiseman's hands and recommended that the whole matter should be dropped. When eventually Cardinal Barnabò heard that Newman had written to Wiseman expressing his willingness to answer any points, he was said to be "thunderstruck", particularly as Wiseman had been in Rome and at the Propaganda and had said nothing of it.

An Oratory school was opened at Edgbaston in 1859, and flourished notwithstanding the fact that it had been the object of false reports. A bishop had expressed dismay on learning that the person to whom he was talking sent his sons to the school, and declared that they did not teach Catholic doctrine there. At the end of 1861, the headmaster and his staff resigned following a dispute in which he had demanded full control over the school and would accept no compromises. Newman appointed replacements and the school was able to reopen in January 1862, with Fr Ambrose St John as headmaster and Newman taking on a number of jobs himself, from teaching to book-keeping. As with all his problems, Newman took a supernatural view of them and resorted first and foremost to prayer. Nevertheless, at this stage his health was suffering and he was forced to take a rest.

Note

[1] Cameron, p. 25 (See Select Bibliography).

6

"Into the Truth"

After the delation of his article about consulting the laity, Newman stopped writing altogether for some years. Then came Charles Kingsley's attack on the truthfulness of the Roman Catholic clergy and on Newman himself. Kingsley[1] had written in *Macmillan's Magazine* that: "Truth, for its own sake, had never been a virtue with the Roman clergy. Father Newman informs us that it need not, and on the whole ought not to be."

Newman had, in fact, said no such thing. The assertion by Kingsley was a complete distortion of what Newman had said in a sermon, preached before he became a Roman Catholic and with no mention of Roman Catholics in it, based on the text: "Behold, I send you out as sheep in the midst of wolves; so be wise as serpents and innocent as doves." (Mt. 10:16)[2]

The correspondence that Newman and Kingsley exchanged was published by Newman in February 1864 together with some reflections by Newman. His defence of Catholic priests against Kingsley's attack was greatly appreciated by them. Kingsley's response to Newman's publication was to write a pamphlet containing more unproven charges.

Newman considered that the best way now for him to respond was to write in detail the history of his religious opinions and set out to show how he had been sincere and honest in holding them. The resulting *Apologia Pro Vita Sua* was originally published section by section over seven weeks. The writing of it was an exhausting operation for Newman, physically, mentally and emotionally. For ten weeks he worked from morning to night, not only writing but having to search for letters he needed to use. On one occasion, he worked right through the night. There was also the enormous anxiety that he should express everything he ought to in the best possible way. The result was a phenomenal success.

If his life had been reminiscent of Job in the Old Testament, the man whom God permitted to be tried by deprivation of all that he possessed, which had virtually happened to Newman after his conversion to Roman Catholicism, so now he was to become like Job in having everything restored, but it was to be a very, very, slow restoration!

The *Apologia* was not an autobiography in the strict sense of the word, nor was it intended to be; to read it as such is to gain only a partial picture of Newman. It traced the development of his religious beliefs from childhood to his conversion to the Roman Catholic faith. It not only restored Newman's integrity in the eye of the general public and cleared him of any intellectual dishonesty but also broke down much of the prejudice hitherto felt against Catholics. Catholics saw Newman as a champion of the Church.

The only people who were not happy were those with Ultramontanist[3] views who tried to get the *Apologia* criticised in Rome because of its final chapter in which freedom of opinion and liberty of thought were strongly defended by Newman. They failed thanks to a defence by the Jesuits of the points made by Newman.

In August 1864, Bishop Ullathorne suggested to Newman that a Catholic Mission might be begun in Oxford. Newman had been offered a suitable site and following the Bishop's proposal he bought the site with financial help from friends, in October, with the hope that an Oratory might be started there. However, on 13 December, in an extraordinary meeting of the hierarchy the bishops rejected the idea of a Catholic college and ruled that parents should be dissuaded from sending their sons to Protestant Universities. The meeting had been called for by the Propaganda Congregation in Rome who had been approached on the matter by Manning who had persuaded Wiseman that Oxford education in any shape or form was a bad thing. Newman sold the site but did buy some houses close to Christ Church in case there was a change of heart and policy. However, Wiseman died in February 1865 and three months later Manning succeeded him as Archbishop of Westminster.

In the spring of 1866 Bishop Ullathorne approached Newman again about the possibility of a Catholic Mission in Oxford. Newman asked that it be agreed by the Propaganda Congregation that the church and house which would comprise the Mission would be an integral part of the Oratory in Birmingham during his life and for three years afterwards. Bishop Ullathorne in writing to the Propaganda included a declaration that he had, in 1864, restrained Newman from taking up educational work at Oxford University. Newman, on seeing a copy of Ullathorne's letter, pointed out the inaccuracy of this statement. When they later met, Ullathorne told Newman he had not written again to the Propaganda about the matter in case it made Newman seem too anxious about the project. The harm that Ullathorne's words to Propaganda had done could be seen in a secret instruction to Ullathorne from the Congregation that, while the Mission could go ahead, Newman was not to live at Oxford. Newman only discovered this later. The general fear was that if Newman did reside at Oxford it would attract young Catholic men to the University, and this was seen as highly undesirable.

Newman had scarcely begun to collect money for the Oxford Mission — unaware at that stage of the instruction about him — when the Prefect of the Propaganda Congregation wrote accusing him of disobedience by preparing boys at the Oratory school for Oxford University. In fact, at this stage the hierarchy had left it to the priests to make the decision as to whether or not a boy should be sent to Oxford. Ullathorne told Newman he should go to Rome and defend himself against the accusation. It was at this time that Ullathorne told Newman of the prohibition on him residing in Oxford — the bishop realised that this was now widely known in Rome, from an article that appeared in the *Weekly Register*.

As the prohibition became known, a number of Catholic laymen publicly protested at the way Newman had been treated. The result of this protest was the infamous correspondence between Manning and Talbot, the English bishops' representative in Rome. Talbot described Newman as "the most dangerous man in England". With regard to the laity and their speaking up in defence of Newman, Talbot wrote to Manning in April 1867:

> They are beginning now to show the cloven foot ["foot" is in Talbot's letter] which I have seen the existence of for a long time. They are only putting into practice the doctrine taught by Dr Newman in his article in *The Rambler*. They wish to govern the Church in England by public opinion. . .
>
> What is the province of the laity? To hunt, to shoot, to entertain? These matters they understand, but to meddle with ecclesiastical matters they have no right at all, and the affair of Newman is a matter purely ecclesiastical. . .[4]

With regard to Newman going to Rome to clear his name, it was eventually agreed at the urging of Ullathorne that Fr Ambrose St John should go on Newman's behalf. He learnt of the cloud that had been hanging over Newman's name in Rome following the delation of his article in *The Rambler* about consulting the laity, and his apparent silence in the face of Propaganda's questions. St John was able to produce a copy of Newman's letter to Wiseman written in 1860. He found out that Talbot had certainly known of the existence of this letter but had said nothing in Newman's defence.

In August 1867 the Propaganda Congregation told the English bishops to send out pastoral letters stating that to attend a non-Catholic university was to place oneself in the proximate occasion of sin. In consequence of this move, Newman withdrew from the Oxford Mission project.

In the meantime, in 1865, Newman had written the immensely popular *Dream of Gerontius*, later set to music by the great English composer, Sir Edward Elgar.[5] The work was dedicated to Fr John Joseph Gordon of the Birmingham Oratory who died in February 1853.

Later in 1865 Newman worked on his *Letter to the Rev. E. B. Pusey DD on his recent Eirenicon*. Published in January 1866, it was a reply to criticisms made by Pusey including an attack on Roman Catholic devotion to Mary. Newman defended Catholic teaching, citing early Church history and writings, and devotion to the Blessed Virgin. With his typical regard for accuracy, for truth, Newman made it clear that not all forms of writing and devotion with regard to the Blessed Virgin were acceptable throughout the Church. He firmly adhered to soundly based official teaching, but at the same time presented that devotion in a very beautiful way. The work was criticised by some but Ullathorne defended Newman's views.

In 1866 Newman received another famous convert to Roman Catholicism: the poet, Gerard Manley Hopkins.

In 1867 Newman received the first of several invitations to participate in the First Vatican Council, but he declined them. When asked if he would be a consultor to the Council's preparatory commission, he said he had never succeeded with boards or committees and always felt out of place on them.

One of Newman's major works, *A Grammar of Assent*, was published in 1870. He had spent two years on the work and described it as at times like tunnelling through a mountain. The work tackled two of the most difficult subjects: how it is possible to believe what cannot be fully understood; and how it is possible to have certitude, inner conviction, even though a thing cannot be demonstrated logically. It was a work of great originality which defended the rationality of believing in Christian revelation.

Newman had long had to deal with a voluminous correspondence from both Catholics and non-Catholics and the good that he was able to do through this apostolate was incalculable. But at no time was his advice and reassurance sought more than at the time of the declaration of the dogma of Papal Infallibility defined by the First Vatican Council in 1870. The extremes sought by the Ultramontanes before the definition and their claims regarding the actual definition caused immense anguish among more moderate Catholics who did not see how they could possibly assent to the extreme views being proposed. Newman, who considered the definition "inexpedient" although he fully accepted it, was able to give reassurance and in his *Letter to the Duke of Norfolk* (1875) set out the accurate teaching regarding infallibility. Ultramontanes were quick to accuse him of lack of loyalty to the Pope, lukewarmness with regard to the faith and so on. But, the Council had been very careful in its wording of the declaration and rejected the formula proposed by ultramontanes.

In the document in which the definition is given, *Pastor Aeternus*, it was firstly the primacy of the Pope which was stressed. The purpose of that primacy was seen as the preservation of unity in the Church. In order to effectively carry out this ministry in the Church, the Pope must have authority. The title of the relevant chapter on infallibility was changed by the Council from the proposed: "On the infallibility of the Roman Pontiff" to "On the infallible teaching office of the Roman Pontiff". The teaching of Vatican I was worded with extreme care. Newman had assured worried Catholics that this would be the case. In a letter written in September 1869 he said:

> If the Church, in the ensuing Council, said anything about Papal Infallibility, it will be so strictly worded, with such safeguards, conditions, limitations, etc. as will add as little as is

conceivable to what is *now* held — it will be so explained and hedged round as not to apply to the case of Honorius etc. It will not be, what Protestants fancy it will be, a declaration that "whatever the Pope says is infallible."[6]

Newman was correct in his estimation of what the Council would say. He was also correct in seeing that, nevertheless, it would be widely misunderstood, even among Catholics themselves.

In Vatican II's *Lumen Gentium*, the teaching of Vatican I regarding the Pope and infallibility was repeated but placed in the wider context of the college of bishops, and in relation to the infallibility to be found in the Church as a whole. (The First Vatican Council had, of course, never been completed; it had had to be suspended because of the Franco-Prussian war.)

On 24 May 1875, Newman's great friend, Fr Ambrose St John died. Those present at his funeral on 29 May recalled the heart-rending sob that Newman gave as he performed the final absolutions. He later spoke of the loss as an open wound which in old men could not be healed.

Two years later there was a joy in his life that he could not have anticipated a few years previously. He was invited to become the first Honorary Fellow of Trinity College, Oxford, the college at which he had matriculated sixty-one years previously. He accepted, with his Bishop's approval, and the following February he made his first visit to Oxford since 1846. He stayed at Trinity College and met his former tutor, Thomas Short. He also met Pusey and paid visits to Oriel and Keble Colleges.

Many people hoped that Newman would be made a Cardinal. Manning was asked by the Duke of Norfolk and the Marquis of Ripon, in July 1878, to communicate this wish to Pope Leo XIII who had succeeded Pius IX earlier in the year. Newman himself knew nothing of this request. Manning wrote to the Cardinal Secretary of State in Rome, supporting the proposal, and the Duke of Norfolk spoke of it himself to the Pope when he visited Rome in the following December.

Manning was asked to find out if Newman would be willing to accept the Cardinalate. This was done through Bishop Ullathorne on 3 February. Ullathorne sent his official reply to Manning stating that the only problem for Newman would be having to live in Rome but this was something that he (Ullathorne) was certain would not be insisted upon by the Pope. Ullathorne enclosed the letter that had been sent to him by Newman requesting that, at his age, he should not have to move from the Oratory to Rome. Manning saw Newman's letter as a refusal of the Cardinalate and sent it to Rome, but did not send Ullathorne's accompanying, explanatory letter. When a report appeared in the *Times* that Newman had turned down the Cardinalate, Newman wrote at once to the Duke of Norfolk denying the report. The Duke wrote to Manning enclosing Newman's letter and Manning at once went to the Pope and explained the misunderstanding. All was well.

There was no need for Newman to live in Rome; he could remain at Birmingham Oratory as he wished.

On 15 May 1879 Newman received the red hat from a delighted Pope Leo who had long greatly admired him. In a speech Newman gave on receiving official notification that he was to be made a Cardinal, he described his life as a never ending battle against the "spirit of liberalism in religion . . . the doctrine that there is no positive truth in religion."[7]

Newman regarded the Cardinalate as a vindication by Divine Providence:

> For twenty or thirty years ignorant or hot-headed Catholics have said almost that I was a heretic. . . On the other hand it had long riled me that Protestants should condescendingly say that I was only half a Catholic, and too good to be what they were in Rome.[8]

He visited Oxford on 5 November where he called on many people. The following year, he stayed from 8-15 May with the Duke of Norfolk, in London, attending the receptions and dinners held in his honour. On 9 May he preached at the Oratory in London. Another visit to Oxford took place on 22-25 May with yet more celebrations to honour him. In 1881, from 25 June to 6 July, he stayed at the London Oratory, preaching there on 26 June.

His writing commitments continued, not without criticism from some people. His article *On the Inspiration of Scripture* was criticised by a Professor of Maynooth College in Ireland.

Like so much else that Newman wrote it was ahead of its time and had yet to be fully appreciated.

Nine months before he died, Newman was called upon to give his considered opinion of a ruling affecting Catholic girls in a large factory. A rule of the place was that the staff should assemble once a day and listen to a Scripture reading followed by an exposition of the reading by the masters, who belonged to the Society of Friends (Quakers). When a priest forbade the girls to attend, the masters requested that Newman's opinion be sought. The aged Cardinal promptly went out in the snow to the factory. The result was that the problem was resolved by setting aside a room in which the girls could recite the Rosary during the prayer assembly time. Newman was delighted at this and declared: "If I can but do work such as that, I am happy and content to live on."[9]

The following month, on Christmas Day, he offered Mass for the last time. He feared that his increasing physical frailty might lead to the chalice being spilt. From then until a few days before he died he repeated the words he had learned by heart of the Mass in honour of the Blessed Virgin, or a Mass for the Dead, each day, with deep love and reverence. He never quite lost the hope that one day he would be well enough to offer Mass properly again.

His poor eye-sight made it necessary to substitute the Rosary for his beloved Breviary. But he loved the Rosary too, regarding it as the most beautiful of devotions, and he was remembered as often having the Rosary in his hand. However, the time came when that also had to be abandoned because of a loss of feeling in his finger-tips.

In his latter years, he was unable to see by candle-light to write or read, which severely curtailed his correspondence. But he welcomed visitors. Particularly welcome was the visit, two days before his death, by his niece, Grace Mozley Langford. This was the daughter of Newman's sister, Harriett, who had become estranged from Newman when he was received into the Roman Catholic Church.

He was suddenly taken ill with pneumonia on 10 August 1890 and died the following evening. He was eighty-nine. Towards the end of his life he repeated his unequivocal belief that: "God has never failed me. He has at all times been to me a faithful God." Of John Henry Newman it can surely be said that he, in turn, was a good and faithful servant of that ever faithful friend.

Newman wrote his own epitaph: "Out of shadows and images into the Truth."[10]

Notes

[1] Charles Kingsley (1819–1875). Church of England clergyman, and Professor of Modern History at Cambridge, he was a well-known novelist whose popular works included: *Westward Ho!* (1855) and *The Water-Babies* (1863).
[2] See *Sermons on Subjects of the Day*, Sermon XX.

3 Ultramontanism favoured the centralization of Church authority. In its extreme form, the attitude was one of being more papal
  than the Pope.
4 E. S. Purcell, *Life of Cardinal Manning*, Vol. II, Macmillan,
  London, 1895, p. 318.
5 Elgar (1857–1934) was given a copy of *Gerontius* in 1889, as a
  wedding present, by Fr T. Knight of St George's Roman Catholic
  church in Worcester, where Elgar had been organist.
6 Letter to Mrs Helbert, 28/9/1869. *LD* XXIV, p. 339.
7 *CP* Vol. VIII, p. 2749.
8 Letter to H. W. Mozley, 25/7/1879. *LD* XXIX, pp. 160–161.
9 *CP* Vol. VI, p. 2198.
10 *Meditations and Devotions*, p. 264.

Section II
An Image of Holiness

7

"Not peace but a sword"

One of the most uncomfortable passages in the Gospels shows Jesus telling his disciples that he has brought not peace but a sword, and going on to speak of the uncompromising first place he must have in the lives of all who follow him:

> Do not think that I have come to bring peace on earth; I have not come to bring peace, but a sword. For I have come to set a man against his father, and a daughter against her mother, and a daughter-in-law against her mother-in-law; and a man's foes will be those of his own household. He who loves father or mother more than me is not worthy of me; and he who loves son or daughter more than me is not worthy of me; and he who does not take his cross and follow me is not worthy of me. (Mt 10: 34–38)

How much more pleasant it is to think of a star-filled sky bringing the angelic song of peace; how much more comfortable and comforting are the words: "Come to me, all who labour and are heavy laden, and I will give you rest. . . For my yoke is easy, and my burden is light." (Mt 11: 28–30)

And yet, the early Christians quickly came to see and experience the fact that Christianity was divisive, like a sword, because it demanded that Christ, the Word of God, and his teaching be given first place in their lives over and above every other consideration. For many in the early Church that meant death, and in the centuries since then martyrs have never been lacking. Not all Christians are called upon to die for their faith; but putting Christ first can often necessitate a choosing that is painful: for some, a kind of living martyrdom. Near our own time the life of John Henry Newman has shown the reality of the "sword" in the life of the Christian. Not long before he became a Roman Catholic he wrote of himself as loving peace but seeming destined to be a man of strife. He was a pilgrim for truth, the truth of Christ. And as he pursued his search he had to choose again and again to put the truth he found before every other consideration. It was a process of growth, one thing leading to another. But, step by step he had to relinquish what he held most dear, including those of his earlier beliefs which he came to regard as containg elements of error and his beloved Oxford; and to endure the estrangement of relatives and friends he had treasured. Both before and after becoming a Roman Catholic he was in the public eye, and suffered much from slander, accusations of hypocrisy, misunderstandings and hostility. For the most part he was silent in the face of false reports, even as Christ was before Pilate and the hostile crowd. He spoke up only when the reports concerned his loyalty and attachment to the Roman Catholic Church. He once said he had thought of making a book of all the statements he had made that he had no intention of leaving the Roman Catholic Church.

Throughout the various trials he suffered and the loss of family and friends, Newman remained fully human. He was sensitive in the best sense of the word; it not only increased his own suffering at times but also enabled him to help others, particularly through the phenomenal number of letters he wrote to both Roman Catholic and non-Roman Catholic correspondents who sought his help. Nor did he cease to love deeply his relatives and friends who turned from him when his path to truth led him to take what many viewed as a treacherous step into Roman Catholicism. His life shows the reality of the "sword" in the lives of those who put the pursuit of Christ, who is the Way, the Truth and the Life, first in their lives at all times. But Newman's life also shows eloquently how to live out this demand of Christ in the light of the supreme commandment to love God and to love our neighbour as ourselves. If there were many who withdrew from Newman when he became a Roman Catholic, he never withdrew his love from them. It takes little imagination to see the heavy cross their loss was to him but he took it up and carried it without bitterness and with total trust in Divine Providence.

He once said:

> Why should we not make any sacrifice, and give up all that is naturally pleasing to us, rather than that light and truth should have come into

the world, yet we not find them? Let us be willing to endure trial and trouble . . .[1]

On another occasion:

From the beginning to the end of Scripture, the one voice of inspiration consistently maintains, not a uniform contrast between faith and obedience, but this *one* doctrine, that the only way of salvation open to us is the *surrender* of ourselves to our Maker in all things — supreme devotion, resignation of our will, the turning with all our heart to God. . .[2]

The surrender, and the ability to accept Christ's words, and to see them as necessary and reasonable, needs a living faith. There must be faith in the awesome mystery of God which is way beyond anything we can imagine; a faith that puts us on our knees in adoration. And there must be faith in the Divinity of Christ; faith in him as the Word of God incarnate. For any mere man, no matter how noble or good he might appear to be, to make the demands that Christ is seen to make with regard to preferring him to all else, would be preposterous, and an outstanding example of megalomania.

One of the most striking things about Newman was his sense of the mystery of God. He was enraptured by it. If one had to choose a single verse or phrase which best captured the spirit of Newman, perhaps there would be no better than his words:

Praise to the Holiest in the height and in the depth be praise.

In all his words most wonderful, most sure in all his ways.

The words, from the *Dream of Gerontius*, as the soul of Gerontius is being taken to the judgement seat of the Divine Saviour, bring to mind the words of St Paul: "O the depth of the riches and wisdom and knowledge of God! How unsearchable are his judgments and how inscrutable his ways." (Rom 11:33) There is an immense beauty in seeing Newman, the intellectual giant and the very practical person, bowing low before the infinite grandeur of God.

He is so bright, so majestic, so serene, so harmonious, so pure; He so surpasses, as being its archetype and fullness, all that is peaceful, gentle, sweet, and fair on earth; His voice is so touching, and His smile so winning while so awful, that we need nothing more than to gaze and listen, and be happy.[3]

Newman's awareness of the awesomeness of God can be seen in the part of the *Dream of Gerontius* where the soul eagerly rushes to meet Christ, as the Guardian Angel exclaims:

Praise to His Name!
The eager spirit had darted from my hold,
And with the intemperate energy of love,
Flies to the dear feet of Emmanuel;
But, 'ere it reaches them, the keen sanctity,
Which with its effluence, like a glory, clothes
and circles round the Crucified has seized,
And scorched, and shrivell'd it; and now it lies

Passive and still before the awful Throne.
O happy, suffering soul! for it is safe,
Consumed, yet quicken'd by the glance of God.

Towards the end of his life, Newman felt particular concern and distress at the increasing disbelief in Christ's Divinity. It was something in which he firmly believed, in the traditional Christian sense of God becoming man: "The Word became flesh" (Jn 1:14).

His belief in the incarnation was enshrined in the *Dream of Gerontius*:

And that a higher gift than grace should flesh and blood refine;
God's presence and his very self, and essence all divine.

Such a life as Newman's makes sense only in the light of faith. In that light his life becomes resplendent; without that light it would be all too easy to see it as one of little more than frustration and wasted talent.

In 1822, Newman had prayed: "O save me from a useless life, keep me from burying my talent in the earth."[4] In 1826, he said: "Teach me, Lord, the value of time, and let me not have lived in vain."[5] But, in 1861, he was having to say: "Whenever I have attempted to do anything for God, I find after a little while that my arms or my legs have a string round them — and perhaps I sprain myself in the effort to move them in spite of it."[6]

He had immense talent and when he joined the Roman Catholic Church he was eager to spend all his time and energy in whatever ways were open to him. One of his greatest trials was to be forced to be inactive, or to have the works he undertook at the request of the bishops fail to come to fruition, because of opposition, misunderstanding, and lack of cooperation — not to mention outright hostility — from others. His trust in Divine Providence was rock solid, and it needed to be. He was convinced that in the end, in God's own time, nothing would be wasted. God's ways were mysterious, but he knew what he was about.

Time and again, even the greatest saints run into the baffling ways that God has of going about things. He seems to try in particular those who set out to follow him closely, or, at least, allow them to be tried. "If this is how you treat your friends, no wonder you have so few of them," was how St Teresa of Avila, a Doctor of the Church, is said to have verbally thumped God during a particularly difficult time.

But why should God try, or permit to be tried, those who wish to follow Christ with their whole mind and heart and will? The answer was being sought to the problem of the suffering of good people long before Christianity came on the world scene. The Book of Job looks at the problem and shows that suffering is not necessarily to be seen as punishment for sin. Job was simply allowed to be tried? Why?[7]

From a worldly point of view there is no satisfactory answer — except perhaps to say there is no God, or if there is one he seems to be just plain nasty at times. Faith starts to give glimpses of an answer. Faith will view this world as Newman viewed it: real enough, but subservient to the far greater reality of the invisible world. Heaven is something for which we have to prepare ourselves, and be prepared by God. It takes little thought to consider whether it is we ourselves or God who knows best how to prepare us. Faith will tell us that God's ways must be best. And yet, being what we are, we tend to judge events in relation to consequences in this life rather than consider them from the point of view of the invisible world which is our real destiny. From the worldly point of view, Christ's life ended in dismal failure but from the real point of view it was total success. Only faith can nod in agreement with that.

It is a very simple fact of life that while we are surrounded by the visible, material world of time and space, we have any number of things to distract us from the invisible world and from God himself. It could be said that God spends our lifetime trying to attract our attention. He stands at the door of our inner, deepest selves, and knocks, and waits. All too often, it seems, we either don't hear or, if we do, are much too busy to do anything about it. But sometimes he finds a ready response, as in Newman. And then what happens? He more often than not acts in the most mysterious of ways which only faith can blindly follow, clinging to trust in Divine Providence.

The most important lesson in this life is for us to learn to love, to give: to go out of ourselves towards God and each other because, faith tells us, that is the life of heaven, the life of the Trinity. The life of the Trinity is an eternal giving of being and love from one to the other, and we are invited to join in that dance of infinite joy to the best of our finite ability. But, somehow, God has to draw us from the selfish end of the spectrum of human nature to the very opposite where we are capable of truly giving and rejoicing in that giving. And it is here on earth that we have to practise what will be made perfect in heaven. God does not force us — there can be no real giving or loving that is forced; there has to be a free choosing to give and to love for it to be genuine.

Like it or not, because of that basic weakness in ourselves that stems from "original sin", we are selfish and rapacious creatures and tend to think of ourselves as the centre of the universe. The tendency can be so subtle at times that we are scarcely, if at all, aware of it. And it is this fundamental selfishness that has to be turned into selflessness if we are to breathe the same air, as it were, as God who is the Infinite Lover, the Infinite Giver.

One could say that the more eager we are to become what God knows we are capable of becoming, the more it seems God will respond with ever more intensive and demanding training. Like a teacher in one of the great arts who knows that a pupil is not only talented but anxious to become more and more skilled in that art, the greatest Teacher of all will correct faults, strengthen weakness and help the pupil to come nearer to perfection. God's would-be saints practise mortification and self-denial, because it strengthens them to become more capable of self-giving to God and others. They nourish themselves on the Eucharist because they know very well that without Christ they can do nothing. These things in turn increase their ability to respond to the demands of the Teacher. Sometimes it seems that God tries us in the very area where we are "weakest", just as the teacher who has the best interests of the pupil at heart will work with that person to eradicate particular weaknesses which are holding back progress: or, conversely, will work to thoroughly polish the unique talents of the individual.

Newman was under no illusions about what the Christian faces:

> I shall be tried: my reason will be tried, for I shall have to believe; my affections will be tried, for I shall have to obey Thee instead of pleasing myself; my flesh will be tried, for I shall have to bring it into subjection.[8]

The way is not easy. To someone who had written to Newman about some particular anxieties, he replied:

> Never mind — go on — "Paradise was not made for cowards" says our St Philip. Call on the Saviour of men — He won't turn a deaf ear to you. He will heal all the wounds which you receive in His service.[9]

He was writing in 1878 and so knew well what he was talking about, after life-long experience. An awareness of the infinite grandeur and majesty of God, and of his infinite lovableness, and faith in the Incarnation. These were the things that drew Newman to correspond with the grace of God to search for religious truth and a life of holiness. If we can glimpse these mysteries and somehow make them truly part of our lives, the uncomfortable passage from the Gospels disappears; to put Christ first is a natural consequence of realising something of who and what he is. Perhaps it is to realise, too, that it is in him that we live and from whom we take our existence. Not to put him first would make as much sense as not to take a breath before saying, "I love you", to a fellow human being: with no breath in us there could be no words, no life. All whom we love and cherish are also in him and the closer we are to him the closer we are to each other.

Perhaps the apparent contradiction in Christ being the Prince of Peace and his words that he had brought not peace but a sword are reconciled at the Last Supper when he said to his disciples: "My peace I leave with you; my peace I give to you; not as the world gives do I give to you." (Jn 14:27)

Those who do turn whole-heartedly to Christ find a peace that cannot be disturbed even if all manner of troubles surround them. The quest for religious truth and his loyalty to that truth in every way, took Newman through many storms and over much rocky ground. The way was not as he had envisaged it in his early years. He had already seen something of the reality when he was visiting Italy in 1833. At

Tre Fontane, traditionally the spot where St Paul was beheaded just outside Rome, Newman wrote a thought-provoking verse:

> Did we but see
> When life first opened, how our journey lay
> Between its earliest and its closing day;
> Or view ourselves as we one time shall be
> Who strive for the high prize, such sight would break
> The youthful spirit, though bold for Jesus' sake.
> But Thou, dear Lord!
> Whilst I traced out bright scenes which were to come,
> Isaac's pure blessedness, and verdant home,
> Didst spare me, and withhold Thy fearful word;
> Wiling me year by year, till I am found A pilgrim pale, with Paul's sad girdle bound.[10]

Thirty years later, speaking of his religious beliefs and his decision to become a Roman Catholic, Newman was able to say:

> I have been in perfect peace and contentment. I never have had one doubt. I was not conscious to myself, on my conversion, of any difference of thought or of temper from what I had before. I was not conscious of firmer faith in the fundamental truths of revelation, or of more self-command; I had not more fervour; but it was like coming into port after a rough sea; and my happiness on that score remains to this day without interruption.[11]

We know from his *Autobiographical Writings*

and his letters that he could feel "down", depressed and frustrated, at the real injustices he suffered. In true humility he knew his capabilities and what he could do for the Church, but he was largely prevented from doing so by people who did not understand, and people who were against him and suspicious of him. Perfect peace? Yes, but not as the world gives. In a letter he wrote in 1841, he said: "There is no truth or peace anywhere, except in Him who is the Truth and has left us His Peace."[12]

As to the rest, Newman loved the writings of St Paul and would surely have echoed his words: "I consider that the sufferings of this present time are not worth comparing with the glory that is to be revealed to us." (Rom 8:18)

Notes

[1] *PPS* Vol. 8, Sermon XIII, p. 199.
[2] *PPS* Vol. 3, Sermon VI, pp. 82–83.
[3] *Discourses to Mixed Congregations*, No. XIV, p. 298.
[4] *Autobiographical Writings*, p. 188.
[5] Ibid., p. 207.
[6] *CP* Vol. VII, p. 2372.
[7] Cf. Dermot Cox, *Man's anger and God's silence. The book of Job*, St Paul Publications, Slough 1989.
[8] *Catholic Sermons*, p. 66. *CP* Vol. IX, p. 3027.
[9] Letter to Miss Tennant, 2/5/1878. *LD* XXVIII, p. 354.
[10] *Verses on Various Occasions*, No. 74, "Our Future", p. 129.
[11] *Apologia*, p. 215.
[12] Letter to Elizabeth Newman, 27/6/1841. *CP* Vol. III, p. 1053.

8

Taking up the cross

If Newman had been emigrating to a distant land with virtually no means of communication between it and the land he was leaving, he could not have been separating himself more from his friends and past life than when he became a Roman Catholic in 1845. It was still a time when to become Roman Catholic was to become something of an outcast; it meant turning from being regarded as a friend into being thought of as an enemy.

Newman was well aware of all that was involved for others while he was in an uncertain state of mind and of the consequences that would follow from a decision to ask to be received into the Roman Catholic Church. In March 1845, seven months before his conversion, he wrote:

> The unsettlement I am causing has been for a long while the one overpowering distress I have had. It is no wonder that through last Autumn it made me quite ill. It is as keen as a sword in many ways, and at times has given me a literal heartache, which quite frightened me.[1]

The following July he wrote in a similar vein:

> This I can say, that my great sorrow has been

the pain and unsettlement of mind I am causing. It is no use talking about it. It has been like a sword through me — but I am getting better now, and almost think the crisis over — though new trials may be coming.[2]

Writing to his sister, Jemima, in March 1845, he listed further implications if he decided to become a Roman Catholic:

At my time of life men love ease — I love ease myself. I am giving up a maintenance involving no duties, and adequate to all my wants; what in the world am I doing this for, (I ask *myself* this) except that I think I am called to do so? I am making a large income by my Sermons. I am, *to say the very least*, risking this; the chance is that my Sermons will have no further sale at all. I have a good name with many; I am deliberately sacrificing it. I have a bad name with more — I am fulfilling all their worst wishes and giving them their most coveted triumph — I am distressing all I love, unsettling all I have instructed or aided; I am going to those whom I do not know and of whom I expect very little — I am making myself an outcast, and that at my age.[3]

His conscience was dictating to him how he should act but the pain of following it was great. It was the thought of losing his beloved friends that he saw as the "great trouble" before him, "and it has not ceased to be, up to this hour, the special sacrifice which I offer up to my Lord and Saviour out of my deep unworthiness as a plea on my behalf when He comes to me in judgement."[4] He was writing in 1861, sixteen years after his conversion.

117

Not the least of his trials as he approached the conviction that he should leave the Anglican Church was the mass of public misunderstanding of his motives, and accusations of lies and deception. He was searching with the utmost care and moving with extreme prudence, and yet around him were flying accusations of already being a Roman Catholic long before he had in fact made the final decision and taken that step.

Perhaps the most poignant letter that Newman wrote in the days before his reception into the Roman Catholic Church was that resigning his Fellowship of Oriel College; the poignancy can be best seen in recalling that day twenty-three years previously when he had just been elected a Fellow.

He had described 12 April 1822 as a turning point in his life. It marked the point where he had risen from "obscurity and need to competency and reputation".[5] He had scarcely dared to hope he would be elected on his first attempt, but he had succeeded and he was grateful to Divine Providence and the Electors for bringing it about. It was a gratitude that extended over the years. What it meant to become a Fellow and the excitement Newman himself felt can be seen in his description of the day on which the news was announced:

The news spread to Trinity with great rapidity. I had hardly been in Kinsey's room a minute, when in rushed Ogle like one mad. Then I proceeded to the President's, and in rushed Ogle again. I find that Tomlinson rushed into Echalaz's room, nearly

118

kicking down the door to communicate the news. Echalaz in turn ran down stairs; Tompson heard a noise and my name mentioned, and rushed out also, and in the room opposite found Echalaz, Ogle and Ward, leaping up and down, backwards and forwards. Men hurried from all directions to Trinity, to their acquaintance there, to congratulate them on the success of their College.[6]

On 3 October 1845, Newman wrote to the Provost: "I shall be obliged to you if you will remove my name from the books of the College and the University."[7]

Newman had loved Oxford and his life there and had been convinced that he would be living until the end of his days within an Oxford College; he relished Littlemore. He took his leave of both in February 1846, four months after his reception into the Roman Catholic Church on 9 October 1845.

He described his departure in the *Apologia*:

I left Oxford for good on Monday, February 23, 1846. On the Saturday and Sunday before, I was in my house at Littlemore simply by myself, as I had been for the first day or two when I had originally taken possession of it. I slept on Sunday night at my dear friend's, Mr Johnson's, at the observatory. Various friends came to see the last of me . . . and I called on Dr Ogle, one of my very oldest friends, for he was my private tutor when I was an undergraduate. In him I took leave of my first college, Trinity, which was so dear to me, and which held on its foundation so many who have been kind to me both when I was a boy, and all through my Oxford life. Trinity has never been unkind to me. There used to be much snapdragon growing on the walls opposite my freshman's rooms there, and I had for years taken it as the emblem of my own perpetual residence even unto death in my University.

On the morning of the 23rd I left the observatory. I have never seen Oxford since, excepting its spires, as they are seen from the railway.[8]

In our more ecumenical times, it is all too easy to forget the attitudes of not so very long ago. Again, it is the words of Newman himself, in 1851, which most graphically describe the experience of being a convert to Roman Catholicism at that time and of the attitudes a convert would encounter:

. . . gradually they drop him, if they do not disown him at once. There used to be pleasant houses open to him, and a circle of acquaintances. People were glad to see him, and he felt himself, though solitary, not lonely; he was by himself, indeed, but he had always a refuge from himself, without having recourse to public amusements which he disliked. It is now all at an end; he gets no more invitations; he is not a welcome guest. He at length finds himself in "Coventry"; and where his presence once was found, now it is replaced by malicious and monstrous tales about him. . . What is his crime? — he is a Catholic among Protestants.[9]

It is little wonder that on another occasion he said it was not an easy thing to prove to people that life could begin anew, and to convince them that "their greatest gain must be counted

120

loss; and that their glory and their peace must be found in what will make them for a while the wonder and the scorn of the world."[10]

All this was clearly very much from his own experience.

Newman's attitude during the painful separations around the time of his conversion was first and foremost one of resignation to God's Will. In the spirit of Job, he blessed God who had given, and who had taken away. In a letter written three days after leaving Oxford, he spoke of the "incomprehensible blessing" of having "Christ in bodily presence in one's house." It swallowed up every other privilege "and destroys, or should destroy, every pain."[11] The "should destroy" is an understandable qualification — Newman was doubtless still feeling the pain of farewells and departures from people and places he had long loved.

But his vision was set to the future. He mentioned in the same letter that on his last morning at Littlemore it was the call of Abraham which was the subject of the lessons in the English Service; the first Office after his arrival at Maryvale had been that of St Matthias, "who took his place in the Apostolate later than his brethren."[12] He was certain that he had made the right move, that he was where God wished him to be, and he was eager to labour in that apostolate.

His cheerfulness at Maryvale was remarked on by a visitor who called in the month after Newman had arrived there, and found him the life of the whole party, keeping everyone cheerful and in good spirits. That could be said to have been the special apostolate that Newman had throughout the rest of his life: keeping people in good spirits by consoling, encouraging, advising; regarding each person as an individual created by God for an eternal destiny. Twenty thousand of the letters he wrote are still in existence and it is estimated that he received between fifty and seventy thousand.

Newman said in his *Second Spring* sermon that it was not God's way that great blessings should come without there being first of all the sacrifice of great sufferings. He was speaking then in relation to the martyrs, but the sacrifices which Newman made may indeed have been the cause of an abundance of blessings for people not only in his life-time but since as people in each generation find for themselves light and peace in his writings.

Notes

[1] Letter to "P", 14/3/1845. *CP* Vol. III, p. 1200.
[2] Letter to Coleridge, 3/7/1847. *CP* Vol. III, p. 1220.
[3] Letter to Jemima, 15/3/1845. *CP* Vol. III, pp. 1205–1206.
[4] Letter to Isaac Williams, 21/10/1861. *LD* XX, p. 60.
[5] *Autobiographical Writings*, p. 63.
[6] Ibid., pp. 62–63.
[7] Letter to the Provost, 3/10/1845, *CP* Vol. III, p. 1232.
[8] *Apologia*, pp. 213–214.
[9] *Lectures on the Present Position of Catholics in England*, p. 192.
[10] *On Certain Difficulties felt by Anglicans*, I, Lecture V, p. 126.
[11] Letter to H. Wilberforce, 26/2/1846. *LD* XI, p. 129.
[12] *CP* Vol. IV, p. 1288.

9

Putting on Christ

What does it mean to put Christ first in every-
day life? It means a deliberate choosing to put
his example, his teaching, his values before
all else — a putting on of Christ. It means
trying to grow more like him in the service of
God. And this can be seen in Newman. There
we see someone who is understanding, kind,
considerate, generous and compassionate. An
unselfish person; a strong person but also a very
gentle person. We see, too, great simplicity and
humility.

To someone who had confided to him that
she no longer felt as fervent as in earlier years,
he wrote:

> Never be afraid, my dear child, of telling any
> weakness to me, because we all have our faults,
> and those who take confessions, of course, hear
> many . . . Do not be disheartened by these in-
> consistencies, whatever they may be, for your
> dear Lord will give you grace to overcome them.

> As time goes on you will know yourself better
> and better. Time does that for us, not only by
> the increase of experience, but by the withdrawal
> of those natural assistances to devotion and self-
> surrender which youth furnishes. When the spirits
> are high and the mind fervent, though we may
> have waywardnesses and perversenesses which we

have not afterwards, yet we have something to battle against them. But when men get old, as I do, then they see how little grace is in them, and how much what seemed grace was but nature. Then the soul is left to lassitude, torpor, dejection, and coldness which is its real state, with no natural impulses, affections or imaginations to rouse it, and things which in youth seemed easy then become difficult. Then it finds how little self-command it has, and how little it can throw off the tempter when he comes behind and places it in a certain direction or position, or throws it down, or places his foot upon it. Then it understands at length its own nothingness, and that it has less grace than it had but it has nothing but grace to aid it. It is the sign of a saint to *grow*; common minds, even though they are in the grace of God, dwindle, (i.e. seem to do so) as time goes on. The energy of grace alone can make a soul strong in age.

Do not then be cast down, if you, though not *very* aged, feel less fervent than you did ten years since — only let it be a call on you to seek grace to supply nature, as well as to overcome it. Put yourself ever fully and utterly into Mary's hands, and she will nurse you and bring you forward. She will watch over you as a mother over a sick child . . .[1]

Writing that letter, in 1850, Newman was clearly speaking from his own personal experience. One of his great attractions is his understanding based on personal experience. Pope Pius XII was convinced that Newman would one day be declared a "Doctor of the Church", a title which has been given to very few in the history of the Christian Church. But,

Newman remains a person who *grew* in holiness; he was no ready-made saint floating through life from beginning to end on a cloud of sanctity, and his own writings left ample evidence of that.

It is generally agreed now that the early autobiographical writings of Newman do not present an attractive picture of him. In part this is due to what he himself later criticised as a "high patronizing tone". He said of his early writing that: "I seldom wrote without an eye to style, and since my taste was bad, my style was bad . . ."[2] He did not destroy his early writings because he wanted it to be seen how mercifully he had been dealt with by God. He left them for reference purposes only, as a truthful record of that early period in his spiritual life. However, he did not consider they were suitable for publication by themselves as they told only part of a long and complex story. Others thought differently and they were published after his death. Whatever picture they may give of Newman as a young man, the fact that he did not mind leaving in existence something that would reflect him in a poor light shows the older Newman to be a person of genuine humility.

The thousands of letters he received are evidence of how widespread was the feeling that Newman would understand whatever problem or difficulty was being put to him; not only that he would understand but that he would invariably be able to offer a remedy or simply well chosen words of comfort and encouragement.

People knew from the many sermons and lectures he gave, and which were later published as books, that here was not only a highly intelligent person but also a deeply spiritual one.

The kindness of Newman went far beyond the writing of letters, although that was an apostolate in itself.

Aubrey de Vere, who lectured at the Catholic University in Dublin, recalled that he had become ill with scarlatina, only a few days after arriving in Newman's house but, "every day, in spite of countless other engagements, Newman found time to sit by my bedside occasionally, and delight me by his conversation"[3]

One area of charitable work that was of particular interest to Newman was that of helping clergy who had converted to Roman Catholicism and were suffering financial hardship as a consequence. One of the effects of being Rector of the University was that Newman was able to find work for convert clergymen in teaching and literature. He delighted in their happiness at this. He saw the establishment of a school connected with the Oratory as providing further possibilities of this kind.

He backed the society newly founded to help convert clergy, but only until he found out that the recipients of the society's aid were being asked to perform particular devotional exercises as a condition for receiving financial aid. He totally disagreed with that policy, later dropped, seeing it as placing an unacceptable burden on the converts who had quite enough to do to get used to their new religion, and he refused to have any further association with the society.

Newman's generosity to others was immense throughout his life, but he was without question very poor in his early years as a Catholic. When he received any money he at once thought only of where it could be sent and who might have need of it.

He relished being able to give £5 or £10 to a person without the recipient knowing what was in the packet, and enjoyed thinking of the surprise when it was opened. The giving was discreet and his main concern was how much he could give them. He saw it as a privilege to give. When someone queried his giving a contribution towards a subscription for some people going to Australia he responded with: "Do you think they won't have appetites when they are landed?"

After his death the *Leicester Post* reported:

> The poor villagers of Rednal knew him not merely by his kind words, but his kindly actions. Every winter he gave to the poor sufficient coal to help them through the cold days and nights; and when the season was more than usually severe, he doubled the amount.[4]

He, in turn, with gentleness and humility, treasured any small gift that was given to him by the poor. One such item was a silk handkerchief which had been left at the door for him by a poor person. Some thirty years later, Newman still had it, and insisted on keeping it with him when he was dying.

The pastoral zeal of the Good Shepherd was to be seen in Newman with regard to a woman who wished to receive instruction in the Catholic Faith but was unable to fix a firm date and had to wait for an opportunity to visit Newman in secret. Newman appreciated her difficult situation and remained at home for many weeks so that he would not run the risk of being out when she called. He refused to be persuaded by those around him that he was over-doing his pastoral zeal and should get out into the fine summer air. His patience was rewarded when the woman was finally able to come to him, was instructed and received into the Roman Catholic Church. She returned to her home country and about three months later Newman received a telegram telling him that she had died unexpectedly in childbirth. He duly used this as a salutary lesson for those who reproached him for staying at home for so long.

A paternal kindness was to be seen on the occasion, in Birmingham, when he noted that two boys who had completed their hour of watching from 3 a.m. to 4 a.m., during a night-watch before the Altar of Repose on Holy Thursday night, remained there for another hour because the watchers for that hour had not arrived. The two boys unaware of Newman's presence, eventually got back to the sacristy to find him waiting for them. He not only praised them for the way they had stayed for two hours instead of one, but also sent them off with strict instructions that they were to be given a good breakfast with plenty of traditional hot cross buns.

A rumour circulated after his death that he had been lacking in generosity when it came to giving away books he had written. This rumour arose from an incident connected with the priestly jubilee of Pope Leo XIII in 1887. It had been proposed that a copy of each book written by English Catholics in the preceding fifty years should be sent to the Pope as a gift. Newman did not wish to have his works included because he considered his best work would give offence due to its being "so flavoured with Protestantism". This was seen as indicating a lack of generosity. Rather, it was humility on Newman's part again. In actual fact he gave away many copies of his books. One publisher complained that he had been over-generous in this respect and thereby spoilt the potential sales figures.

Suffering and bereavement showed Newman at his most compassionate but always with words designed to strengthen the faith of those suffering and give them courage to take up their cross.

To one person who was suffering he wrote, in 1854:

> Don't doubt, nor do you, that you will be supported through everything. Recollect when God gives faith, and strength, he tries them. He does not give them for nothing, or, as it were, for ornaments, but for use. It is the solemn privilege of those who have more gifts that they have more suffering.[5]

To someone who had lost a 21-year-old son he wrote:

Let me bear witness, not only as a matter of faith,

129

which we all receive, but as a point, which the experience of life has ever been impressing on me, more and more deeply, from my early youth down to this day, that unusual afflictions, coming on religious persons, are proofs that they are the objects, more than others, of the love of God. Those whom He singularly and especially loves, He pursues with His blows, sometimes on the same wound, till perhaps we are tempted to cry out for mercy . . .[6]

To a person whose wife was dying, he wrote words in which all who are fearing an imminent bereavement can find comfort and strength:

It has truly grieved me to hear of the severe trial you are under, though really such trials are our portion. I think one may say it without exaggeration, but (sic) they who seek God do (as it were) come for afflictions. It is the way He shows His love, and to keep from so doing is His exception . . . You are called to trouble as we all are, and the severer the more God loves you. He may mercifully consider your present distress and suspense sufficient for His inscrutable purposes — if so it will come to an end with nothing more. But anyhow be sure He does not willingly afflict us, nor will put a single grain's weight more suffering than it is meet and good for you to bear — and be sure that with your suffering your support will grow, and that if in His great wisdom and love He take away the desire of your eyes, it will only be to bring her really nearer to you. For those we love are not nearest to us when in the flesh, but they come into our very hearts as being spiritual beings, when they are removed from us.[7]

The first close bereavement had come to Newman in his early years with the death of his beloved sister, Mary. The last major bereavement he had to undergo was that of his close friend and fellow Oratorian, Fr Ambrose St John, in 1875. He spoke of it as "the heaviest affliction I have had in my life."[8] It was, he said, "an open wound, which in old men cannot be healed."[9] Those who attended St John's funeral never forgot the sudden sob which Newman gave at one point in the ceremony.

He encouraged people not to doubt the loving providence of God at times of bereavement, but he was well aware of the pain involved and the long-lasting nature of that pain:

> This I have observed, that such dreadful blows do issue in great blessings, and when we look back upon them years afterwards, we see what mercy there is in them . . . This is after the wound is healed, but oh! how long it will be in healing.[10]

He was writing two years after the death of Fr Ambrose St John. But he never forgot what lay beyond death and to one nun who was thought to be close to death he wrote: "You are to be envied not lamented over, because you are going to your own Lord and God, your Light, your Treasure, and your Life."[11]

Those who knew him were impressed by his simplicity and modesty. His presence was impressive and his sermons, given without gestures and dramatic expressions, could and did move people to tears because he made them aware of the Divine Presence among them, but he was

131

in no way overbearing. He was as at home in a friend's house balancing two small children on his knees as gliding into a pulpit to preach.

His diligent search for truth could perhaps only have been undertaken by a person of deep humility because it meant admitting to the possibility of being wrong and of giving up or amending views when his search led him to discern errors. But the greatest test of his humility could be said to have come with his conversion to Roman Catholicism. It was one thing for Fr Dominic to tell Newman and his fellow-converts that they were but babes in the faith, another thing to live through that early stage. But Newman accepted the treatment he received: being questioned publicly on the catechism in the church at Maryvale; having to wait in a queue of schoolboys to make his confession to Dr Wiseman, and sitting with young students at lectures in Rome.

In Rome he had been happy to elucidate his ideas contained in his *Essay on the Development of Christian Doctrine*, when some concern was expressed over it. His willingness to explain and to submit his writings and views to ecclesiastical authority remained throughout his life.

It was one of the bitter ironies in Newman's life that when his article *On Consulting the Faithful* rang all manner of alarm bells in Rome, the questions which the authorities asked to be put to him, by Cardinal Wiseman, Archbishop of Westminster, were never forwarded to him. The result was that for some years he was under a cloud in Rome. With regard to any unjust treatment he received from the authorities, or false accusations from elsewhere, his attitude was stated in a letter he wrote to one person who thought he should speak up and defend himself:

> As to defending myself, you may make yourself quite sure I never will, unless it is a simple duty. Such is a charge against my religious faith — such against my veracity — such any charge in which the cause of religion is involved . . . I consider that Time is the great remedy and Avenger of all wrongs, as far as this world goes.[12]

He took as his models in this two particular saints: St Philip Neri and St Joseph Calasanctius, both of whom had had to endure similar misunderstandings and treatment. He even tended to make light of these things, saying that "compared with ill health, with the loss of friends, or with poverty, it weighs as nothing." He added: "Therefore I have nothing to complain of, nothing to wish otherwise, everything to rejoice at."[13]

A particularly beautiful picture of Newman's humility comes from near the end of his life. When the Bishop of Birmingham, Dr Ullathorne, was retiring in August 1887, he visited Newman and wrote afterwards that he had found him "much wasted but very cheerful." As Ullathorne left, Newman asked him for "a great favour". When the Bishop asked him what it was, Newman knelt down, bowed his head and asked for a blessing. The blessing was given as Ullathorne laid his hand on Newman's head and said, "My dear Lord

133

Cardinal, notwithstanding all the laws to the contrary, I pray God to bless you, and that His Holy Spirit may be full in your heart." Walking to the door with the Bishop, Newman refused to put on his biretta, as would have been customary, saying to him, "I have been indoors all my life, whilst you have battled for the Church in the world."

Ullathorne commented afterwards that he had felt annihilated in Newman's presence, "There is a Saint in that man."[14]

Notes

[1] Letter to Miss Holmes, 31/7/1850. *LD* XIV, pp. 28–29.
[2] *Autobiographical Writings*, p. 149.
[3] *Recollections of Aubrey de Vere*, London, 1907, p. 268 (quoted in *CP* Vol. IV, p. 1385).
[4] *Leicester Post*, 20/8/1890. *CP* Vol. XVI, p. 5785.
[5] Letter to Mrs J. W. Bowden, 30/3/1854. *LD* XVI, p. 96.
[6] Letter to Lady Giorgiana Fullerton, 4/6/1855. *LD* XVI, p. 476.
[7] Letter to H. Manning, 14/7/1837. *LD* VI, p. 95.
[8] Letter to W. Leigh, 5/6/1875. *LD* XXVII, p. 313.
[9] Letter to Miss Holmes, 10/9/1875. *LD* XXVII, p. 352.
[10] Letter to Mrs William Froude, 2/9/1877. *LD* XXVIII, p. 235.
[11] Letter to Sr. M. Gabriel du Boulay, 15/5/1876. *LD* XXVIII, p. 63.
[12] Letter to Emily Bowles, 8/1/1867. *LD* XXIII, p. 16.
[13] Letter to Miss A. Aungier, 24/4/1867. *LD* XXIII, p. 188.
[14] *CP Volumen Unicum*, p. 117.

10

"As I have loved you"

The person who puts Christ first in his or her life will be someone who tries at all times to love others as he did: "This is my commandment, that you love one another as I have loved you." (Jn 15:12)

That love will embrace both friend and enemy, in accordance with Christ's teaching and example. In Newman we can see someone who fully lived out this aspect of the Gospel, this consequence of putting Christ and his teaching first in our lives. Newman pointed out that Christ had chosen to be born of a human mother in order to:

. . . put honour on all those earthly relations and connections which are ours by nature; and to teach us that, though He has begun a new creation, He does not wish us to cast off the old creation, as far as it is not sinful.

Hence it is our duty to love and honour our parents, to be affectionate to our brothers, sisters, friends, husbands, wives, not the less, but even more, than it was man's duty before our Lord came on earth.

As we become better Christians, more consistent and zealous servants of Jesus, we shall become only more and more anxious for the good of all around us . . . And this we shall do from the recollection of how our Lord loved His Mother . . .

We then on earth must feel a tender solicitude for all our relatives, all our friends, all whom we know or have dealings with. And, moreover, we must love not only those who love us, but those who hate us or injure us, that we may imitate Him, who not only was loving to His Mother, but even suffered Judas, the traitor, to kiss Him, and prayed for His murderers on the Cross.[1]

Newman was certainly a loving son and brother in his family and did a great deal to help them financially after his father's bankruptcy, including paying for his brother, Frank, to attend Oxford University. He took time to give plenty of practical advice when his mother and sisters moved to Brighton after his father's death. Newman himself made all the arrangements with regard to wallpapering and furnishing the house. His letters to his family show his affection for them.

One of the most attractive things about Newman was his attitude towards friendship, and the way he treasured his friends. He possessed a natural gift for friendship and few people can have placed it more beautifully in a Christian setting than he. In a sermon preached on the feast of St John the Beloved Disciple, Newman spoke of Jesus' friendship with the Saint. It showed, he said, not only that Christ was fully human in his needs and feelings but also that:

> there is nothing contrary to the spirit of the Gospel, nothing inconsistent with the fulness of Christian love, in having our affections directed in an especial way towards certain objects,

towards those whom the circumstances of our past life, or some peculiarities of character, have endeared to us.

He spoke of such friendships as being "the best preparation for loving the world at large, and loving it duly and wisely . . ." The ever-practical Newman dismissed the idea that it was in some way possible to love the whole world without having learnt to love individual people placed near to us in the course of daily life.

> The real love of man *must* depend on practice, and therefore, must begin by exercising itself on our friends around us, otherwise it will have no existence.[2]

Newman's close friends included several women, and, like many of the great saints, he did not see this friendship as being in any way incompatible with his dedication to Christ through celibacy. This attitude is becoming more widespread in the late 20th century but, in Newman's time, it was not so usual. In this matter, perhaps Newman's close relationship with his sisters did much to contribute towards his ability to form friendships with women. One friend, Emily Bowles, who was devoted to Newman, left a delightful picture of him as a host and a friend.

At the end of May 1866, she had gone to Edgbaston at Newman's invitation to see a play performed by the Oratory School. The next day she attended Mass and lunch with other guests at Rednal. She desribed the occasion:

> Everything was bright, gay with flowers, and

festive with delightful conversation; the Father (Newman) himself attending to the guests and providing for their accommodation and comfort until absolutely forced by Father Ambrose with playful violence to keep his seat and take his own food.

After the meal some of the guests organised a walk over a nearby hill which enjoyed views over the countryside. Emily Bowles relates:

To my infinite joy, for I had thought important guests would have claimed him, the Father came to say that he was going to walk over the hill with me. . . . I recall still each moment of it, every step of the way, every look and tone of the Father as we passed along the bilberry-bordered path, or under the fragrant firs, where the ground was carpeted with their brown needles and strewed with cones. I remember his stopping with finger upraised at an opening, as the breeze brought the sound of far-off bells, and as we looked over what seemed a boundless stretch of blue distance, he spoke of the necessity of human life and its claims and interests coming in ever to make up the whole beauty of the picture or the poem, whichever you choose to call it, that a wide outlook creates. The winter had been long, and the spring lingering and late, and I remember speaking of the joy, the bound of the heart that the green and flowery flush gave me after the winter's real pain. "Yes," he said, "it is so. After a long winter such as we have had, spring is like the perpetual miracle of Aaron's rod budding — Death is swallowed up in victory." To this day I never see the chesnuts (sic) putting out their fans and flowery spikes without recalling those words and the voice that said them.[3]

With regard to Newman's attitude towards other people, much has been written and said about his "sensitivity." The word is used to mean touchy, easily offended and hurt. His reputation in this is not deserved and originally arose from gossip and false reports that emerged in London at the time of the dispute between Newman and Faber over a matter of principle affecting their respective Oratories, in Birmingham and London. Characteristically, Newman had remained silent in public and imposed silence on his fellow-Oratorians in Birmingham in order not to harm the immense amount of good work which Faber was doing in London and which Newman recognised and appreciated. He considered it the lesser evil to allow himself to be misrepresented and misunderstood. That is heroism, not "sensitivity."

This is not to say that Newman was lacking in sensitivity in the sense of being fully human with deep emotions and capable of being hurt by the frustrations he often had to face and the betrayals of trust he encountered. Those who prefer their saints to come leather-bound, in rhinoceros hide, have not come across any real saints. Saints are first and foremost human beings with the attributes, weaknesses and potentiality of all human beings. Humanity is the raw material from which grace draws sanctity. No raw material, no sanctity. Anyone who wishes to have saints with eyes

139

cast heavenwards scarcely noticing the problems and pain of living on earth had better stick to plaster statues, not real saints.

Newman was prudent and realistic in his dealings with others. When, for sound reasons, he felt he could no longer trust someone, he bore them no personal animosity. Any betrayal of trust was painful to him, as it was to Christ himself, but, like Christ, he forgave the injustice and injuries.

After lengthy experience, Newman came to the conclusion that he could not rely on Faber. In November 1860 he wrote, "He has a thousand attractive points, but he has a restless spirit of intrigue which nothing can quench . . ."[4]

Three years later he described Faber as "a person of great natural gifts, and of high aspirations, and of an impulsive affectionateness. His great fault was that he was not the same man two days running — you could never be sure of him."[5]

Newman's attitude towards Faber was tolerant and forbearing. He was patient as well as firm in insisting on the principle of the autonomy of each Oratorian house. His attitude had been the same with regard to earlier difficulties, whether it was over St Wilfrid's, the setting up of an Oratory in London, or subsequent difficulties between Faber and the London Oratorians.

Newman was well aware of the defamatory talk about himself that emanated from the London Oratorians including Faber, and yet his personal attitude to Faber can be seen in his going to see him when he was seriously ill in July 1863, and attending his funeral in the following September. It can be seen still more in the fact that Newman attributed the success of his *Apologia* to the prayers of the deceased Faber, and asked for one of Faber's hymns to be sung when he was recovering from a near fatal fall in 1888. The hymn was the *Eternal Years* and Newman compared his own hymn, *Lead Kindly Light*, unfavourably with it:

> Some people have liked my *Lead Kindly Light* and it is the voice of one in darkness, asking for help from our Lord. But this is quite different; this is one with full light, rejoicing in suffering with our Lord, so that mine compares unfavourably with it. This is what those who like *Lead Kindly Light* have got to come to — they have to learn it.[6]

Newman deliberately stayed away from the opening of the Brompton Oratory church, in London, because he did not wish by his presence on so formal an occasion to appear to be exercising some form of generalate over the London Oratorians. However, he attended Vespers and preached at the London Oratory on 9 May 1880; and the following year he stayed there from 25 June to 6 July, preaching on 26 June.

Another person whom Newman came reluctantly to distrust was Henry Manning, who succeeded Wiseman as Archbishop of Westminster. Manning was outwardly friendly and well-disposed towards Newman and yet acted in a very different way behind his back. Such, for

141

example, was the case over Newman's *Letter to Pusey*, published in 1866. Newman received two letters from Manning in which the *Letter* was praised, but Newman soon learnt from his own Bishop, Dr Ullathorne, that Manning was in fact trying to get parts of the *Letter* censured. In speaking of Manning's attitude towards him, Newman wrote to a close friend, in 1866:

> If you ask my explanation of all this, I don't impute to him any animosity to me — but I think he is of a nature to be determined to *crush* or to *melt* every person who stands in his way. He has views and is determined to carry them out — and I must either go with him or be annihilated. I say this, because he long wished to get me made a Bishop (in partibus) — I believe because he knew it would be (as it were) putting me "in the House of Lords". When he found that I should not accept the offer, as feeling it would interfere with my independence, his only remaining policy is to put me out.[7]

To another friend he had written:

> You strangely misunderstood what I said about Manning, and treated it as if it denoted personal feeling on my part. What I said was, that I could not trust him — "confidence" is the word I used. Confidence is an intellectual habit, not a moral . . . I repeat to *you*, what I should not say to everyone, viz. I never can trust he has not an *arrière pensée* in any profession or offer he makes. It is not my feeling alone; I have long defended him; I am one of the last who have given into it.[8]

Correspondence between Manning and Mgr

George Talbot who represented the English bishops in Rome, shows the type of enmity that Newman had to face. In one such letter to Manning, criticising Newman's *Letter to Pusey*, Talbot said: "You will have battles to fight, because every Englishman is naturally anti-Roman. To be Roman is to an Englishman an effort." Talbot concluded: "Dr Newman is more English than the English. His spirit must be crushed."[9]

Manning had replied:

> What you write about Dr Newman is true. Whether he knows it or not, he has become the centre of those who hold low views about the Holy See, are anti-Roman, cold and silent, to say no more, about the Temporal Power, national, English, critical of Catholic devotions, and always on the lower side.[10]

Needless to say, Manning, like Talbot, held extreme Ultramontanist views and as such considered every other, more moderate, view as disloyalty to the Holy See and showing a lack of true Roman Catholic spirit. Similar views were held by Faber and the London Oratorians, and this had contributed to the alienation that arose between the Birmingham and London Oratories. Mgr Talbot did much to harm Newman's reputation in Rome but Newman's attitude towards him can be seen in the letter he wrote to him in 1867:

> I received with much satisfaction the report which Fr St John has given me of your conversation with him. I know you have a good heart;

I know you did me a good service in the Achilli matter — and you got me a relic of St Athanasius from Venice which I account a great treasure; and for those reasons I have been the more bewildered at your having of late years taken so strong a part against me, without (I may say) any real ground whatever; or rather I *should* have been bewildered, were it not that, for now as many as thirty-four years, it has been my lot to be misrepresented and opposed without intermission by one set of persons or another. Certainly, I have desiderated in you, as in many others, that charity which thinketh no evil, and have looked in vain for that considerateness and sympathy which is due to a man who has passed his life in attempting to subserve the cause and interests of Religion, and who, for the very reason that he has written so much, must, from the frailty of our common human nature, have said things which had better not have been said, or left out complements and explanations of what he *has* said, which had better been added. I am an old man, perhaps within a few years of my death, and you can now do me neither good nor harm. I have never been otherwise than well disposed towards you. When you first entered the Holy Father's immediate service, I used to say Mass the first day of every month, that you might be prospered at your important post; and now I shall say Mass for you seven times, beginning with this week, when you are keeping the Feast of St Philip, begging him at the same time to gain for you a more equitable judgment of us and a kinder feeling towards us on the part of our friends, than we have of late years experienced.[11]

144

Notes

[1] *Meditations and Devotions*, pp. 221–222.
[2] *PPS* Vol. 2, Sermon V, p. 55.
[3] *CP* Vol. VII, pp. 2519–2520.
[4] Letter to James Hope Scott, 28/11/1860. *LD* XIX, p. 427.
[5] Letter to Miss Holmes, 20/11/1863. *LD* XX, p. 560.
[6] *CP* Vol. IV, p. 1484.
[7] Letter to Charlotte Wood, 21/12/1866. *CP* Vol. VI, p. 2003.
[8] Letter to T. W. Allies, 4/6/1865. *LD* XXI, p. 483.
[9] E. S. Purcell, *Life of Cardinal Manning*, Vol. II, Macmillan, London, 1895, p. 323.
[10] Ibid, pp. 322–323.
[11] *CP* Vol. VI, pp. 2240–2241, and p. 2315.

11

Devotional balance

Towards the end of his novel *Loss and Gain*,
Newman describes the principal character's
encounter with the service of Benediction of the
Blessed Sacrament, in a Roman Catholic
church:

> A cloud of incense was rising on high; the peo-
> ple suddenly all bowed low; what could it mean?
> the truth flashed on him, fearfully yet sweetly;
> it was the Blessed Sacrament — it was the Lord
> Incarnate who was on the altar, who had come
> to visit and to bless his people. It was the Great
> Presence, which makes a Catholic church dif-
> ferent from every other place in the world; which
> makes it, as no other place can be, holy.[1]

This sense of mystery and reverence were, of
course, Newman's own. The Eucharist was at
the centre of his life. Even before becoming a
Roman Catholic or accepting the Real Presence
of Christ in the Eucharist, he had deplored the
lack of reverence which he considered the
undergraduates showed at the time of their College Communion. Years later, as a Roman
Catholic, he said, "In times of great trouble,
when you think everything is gone from you,
if you have with you our Lord in the Blessed
Sacrament you have still everything — whatever

you have lost, if you have not lost Him, you have lost nothing."[2]

The annual feast of *Corpus Christi*, celebrating the presence of Christ in the Blessed Sacrament, and the devotion of the Forty Hours exposition of the Blessed Sacrament, were occasions he especially loved.

Newman fully lived the rich devotional life available to him in the Roman Catholic Church. His dedication to religious truth can be seen in the doctrinal soundness of his devotion. He disliked and deplored distortions and exaggerations, nor would he give support to new or little known devotions, partly because he did not wish to give the impression of having an authority which he did not have and partly because he did not wish in any way to prejudice any discussion that might take place in the appropriate tribunal.

His relationship with his Creator came before all else and above all else. In Newman there is a beautiful balance between awareness of the infinite majesty, the complete "otherness" of God, and the belief that no one and nothing is closer to each individual human being. With faith he accepted the mysteries of the Trinity, the Incarnation and the Eucharist. He did not believe that one could simply reason one's way into faith. Reason certainly had to be used in the search for truth, but along with that there had to be prayer, for guidance and the light of faith. In that light the great mysteries of the faith could be adored as mysteries.

Especially dear to Newman was the mystery

of the Incarnation: the Word of God, the second person of the Blessed Trinity, taking human flesh, human nature. For this reason, he loved the shrine of the Holy House at Loreto, venerated as the house from Nazareth, because of its association with the Incarnation. At Christmas he loved to kneel in silence before the crib. He regarded the Incarnation as the greatest of all miracles and could see no difficulty in accepting other, lesser, miracles if one accepted that.

Newman's deep sense of awe at the mystery of God was combined with complete trust in Divine Providence. He was able to say:

> O Lord, here I am. I will be whatever Thou wilt ask me. I will go whithersoever Thou sendest me. I will bear whatever Thou puttest on me. Not in my own might or my own strength. My strength is very weakness; if I trust in myself more or less, I shall fail — but I trust in Thee. I trust and I know that Thou wilt aid me to do, what Thou callest on me to do. I trust and I know that Thou wilt never leave me nor forsake me . . .[3]

So much confidence did he have in prayer and Divine Providence that people sometimes thought he was unconcerned about events which had, in fact, given him much pain. Whatever was the outcome after prayer he accepted as God's answer. To others, Newman would say, "What more did you look for; was it not to do as God willed that we were praying?"[4]

He was always deeply touched and grateful when others remembered him in their prayers. Any important work to be undertaken, any major decision to be made, was always preceded by much prayer on Newman's part: the Mass, novenas and litanies.

His reverence for the things of God made it important to him that every sacred ceremony should be carried out perfectly and that the sanctuary should be appropriately decorated. He encouraged those involved in the preparations and praised them afterwards. If anyone was careless in genuflecting to the Blessed Sacrament, Newman would quietly tell them about their lack of reverence. On one occasion, when he had not been able to kiss the crucifix properly when it was presented to him during a ceremony, he requested that it again be given to him afterwards so that he might kiss it with due reverence.

With regard to the closeness in the relationship between the individual soul and its Creator, he said:

> . . . the Catholic Church allows no image of any sort, material or immaterial, no dogmatic symbol, no rite, no sacrament, no saint, not even the Blessed Virgin herself, to come between the soul and its Creator. It is face to face, "solus cum solo", in all matters between man and his God. He alone creates; He alone has redeemed; before His awful eyes we go in death; in the vision of Him is our eternal beautitude.[5]

On another occasion, he said that non-Roman Catholics often misunderstood the Church's teaching regarding the Blessed Virgin, not realising that:

> He "in whom we live, and move and are", who

149

new-creates us with His grace, and who feeds us with His own Body and Blood, is closer to us and more intimately with us than any creature; that Saints and Angels, and the Blessed Virgin herself, are necessarily at a distance from us, compared with Him . . .[6]

On the same theme, in his *Letter to Pusey*, Newman wrote:

He alone has an entrance into our soul, reads our secret thoughts, speaks to our heart, applies to us spiritual pardon and strength. On Him we solely depend. He alone is our inward life . . . He is ever renewing our new birth and our heavenly sonship. In this sense He may be called, as in nature, so in grace, our real Father.

Mary is only our adopted mother, given us from the Cross; her presence is above, not on earth; her office is external, not within us. Her name is not heard in the administration of the Sacraments. Her work is not one of ministration towards us; her power is indirect. It is her prayers that avail, and they are effected by the fiat of Him who is our all. Nor does she hear us by any innate power, or any personal gift, but by His manifestation to her of the prayers which we make her.[7]

Newman's love for Christ was reflected in his devotion to the Sacred Heart. It was a devotion which he described as affecting him more powerfully than any other. He had a deep love for the Passion of Christ and a favourite book during Passiontide was the *Life of Our Lord Jesus Christ* by Father Thomas of Jesus. Even on the Good Friday before he died, Newman was able to make the customary genuflections as he approached the Cross to venerate it. The meditations he wrote for the Way of the Cross are still frequently used during Lent and Holy Week.

It had always been his heartfelt hope that in his final years he would be able to devote his time entirely to reading and studying the Scriptures. This was not possible but throughout his life he meditated on them. He was happy when the Office of the day included more psalms and readings than usual, even when he was particularly busy. He liked to meditate on the Book of Job, and he knew the Books of Ezekiel and Isaiah by heart. When his eyesight failed he had the Gospels and Letters read to him each day. He was a critical listener — pointing out the correct emphasis and picking up any mispronunciations.

Some people complained that his sermons were too full of the Scriptures, but others were moved to tears by his reading of scriptural passages. One woman said: ''While the Cardinal was reading the Epistle I was so overcome by the way in which he read it I felt I needed no sermon and it made me cry so much that I looked aside to be sure that no one was observing me. But I found everyone round about me crying also.''[8]

Few people can have spoken so tenderly and appreciatively of the Blessed Virgin as Newman did, nor so well defended the tradition of devotion to her and its desirability. He was not happy with certain manifestations of this devotion but said, ''I trust I do not love her the less, because I cannot enter into them.''[9] One has only to glance at his Meditations for the month of May to see that his love for her was great indeed. But it was always set in the framework of doctrinal soundness:

> Let no one for an instant suppose that she is not supremely zealous for His honour, or, as those who are not Catholics fancy, that to exhalt her is to be unfaithful to Him. Her true servants are still more truly His. Well as she rewards her friends, she would deem him no friend, but a traitor, who preferred her to Him. As He is zealous for her honour, so is she for His. He is the Fount of grace, and all her gifts are from His goodness. O Mary, teach us ever to worship thy Son as the One Creator, and to be devout to thee as the most highly favoured of creatures.[10]

Newman was a true servant of Mary. He dearly loved the Rosary and regarded its great power to be in turning the Creed into a prayer that brought the great truths of Christ's life and death nearer to people's hearts. When the Pope established the custom of the public recitation of the Rosary throughout October, Newman enthusiastically introduced this October devotion at the Oratory.

Among the verses that Newman wrote was one to his Guardian Angel and included the lines:

> My oldest friend, mine from the hour
> When first I drew my breath;
> My faithful friend, that shall be mine,
> Unfailing, till my death.[11]

Newman could see no difficulty in accepting

the existence of angels. "Was not the animal kingdom in fact every bit as mysterious as anything the Scriptures said about angels?" he asked. We were connected to that animal world, without understanding it; where was the difficulty in accepting our connection with a world of beings superior to humankind?

Newman had a great devotion to, and trust in, the saints and their intercession. Foremost among them, of course, was St Philip Neri, who established the Oratory in Rome. He also placed much confidence in St Anthony of Padua, and the saint was given the onerous task of finding the witnesses that Newman desperately needed during the Achilli trial. He did! St Francis de Sales was another of Newman's favourites and he dedicated the private chapel he had, following his being made a cardinal, to this saintly bishop and Doctor of the Church.

Newman had a particular devotion to St Athanasius renowned for his defence of Christ's Divinity. Visiting the saint's shrine in Venice, he was so absorbed in prayer that he was unable later to describe the surrounding area. He regarded his conversion to the Roman Catholic Church as having been due to studying the writings of St Athanasius. St John Chrysostom and Tertullian were also among Newman's favourites. He spoke of Tertullian as *the* theological genius in the early Church.

The practical nature of Newman, and his love for truth and solidly based devotion, can be seen in his words about saints. His wit and humour come through as well.

I confess to a delight in reading the lives, and dwelling on the characters and actions of the Saints of the first ages, such as I receive from none besides them; and for this reason, because we know so much more about them than about most of the Saints who come after them. People are variously constituted; what influences one does not influence another. There are persons of warm imaginations, who can easily picture to themselves what they never saw. They can at will see Angels and Saints hovering over them when they are in church; they see their lineaments, their features, their motions, their gestures, their smile or their grief. They can go home and draw what they have seen, from the vivid memory of what, while it lasted, was so transporting. I am not one of such; I am touched by my five senses, by what my eyes behold and my ears hear. I am touched by what I read about, not by what I myself create. As faith need not lead to practice, so in me mere imagination does not lead to devotion. I gain more from the life of our Lord in the Gospels than from a treatise *de Deo*. I gain more from three verses of St John than from the three points of a meditation.[12]

Newman said he wanted to hear a saint converse; he was not content to look at a statue. That, he said, was why he exulted in the writings of the Fathers. It was a saint's writings that were for Newman the real "life" of the saint. Rather than read about such things as visions, prophecies, meditations and miracles in the lives of saints, he said he would prefer to have an action or event in the person's life looked at in detail, with the saint's own comments on it. He wanted to see not only saintly acts but also the saintly moves behind them.

The devotional life of Newman was built on firm foundations. There was, through it all, a great simplicity. He never drew attention to himself, never used extravagant gestures. After he had been made a cardinal, he looked hopefully in the *Caeremoniale* to see if he could correctly appear in church in black rather than red; he felt so conspicuous in his cardinal's red.

Throughout that devotional life there also runs the note of trust: trust in Divine Providence; trust in the intercession of Mary and the Saints. It could be summed up in Newman's words: "We are in His hands — and cannot be in better.[13]

Notes

[1] *Loss and Gain*, p. 294.
[2] *CP* Vol. IV, p. 1465 (first sermon preached after the death of Fr Ambrose St John).
[3] *Catholic Sermons*, pp. 65–66. *CP* Vol. VIII, p. 2958.
[4] Papers of Fr William Neville, Vol. II. *CP* Vol. VI, p. 2201.
[5] *Apologia*, p. 183.
[6] *Discourses to Mixed Congregations*, No. IX, p. 179.
[7] *Letter to Pusey*, pp. 89–90.
[8] Papers of Fr William Neville, Vol. II. *CP* Vol. VI, p. 2231.
[9] *Apologia*, p. 183.
[10] *Meditations and Devotions*, pp. 148–149.
[11] *Verses on Various Occasions*, No. 166, 'Guardian Angel'. pp. 296–298.
[12] *Historical Sketches*, Vol. II, p. 217.
[13] Letter to Lady Giorgiana Fullerton, 4/6/1855, *LD* XVI, p. 476.

12

Newman today

Newman's importance as an ecumenical figure is clear. His life, work and attitudes contributed greatly to a better understanding between Roman Catholics and other Christians in his own day and continue to be of immense importance today. His commitment to religious truth; his charity towards those who sincerely held beliefs other than those he came to regard as true; his willingness to help those who turned to him with doubts and queries, regardless of which ecclesial communion they belonged to; his diligent explanation of the true Roman Catholic teaching; and the deep spirituality of much of his writing which can be savoured by Christians in general, and, indeed, those of other religions — all these aspects make him not only an important figure in himself, but also provide an outstanding example for all who wish to advance the cause of unity.

He has been inaccurately described as a Pied Piper, leading thousands of Anglicans into the Roman Catholic Church. Such a description belies the care and caution he advised when would-be Roman Catholic converts approached him. He became a Roman Catholic because, after years of prayer and study, he came to the conclusion that that was where God wanted him to be. While he sincerely hoped that others might come to the same conclusion, he in no way became the sort of catalyst that the Roman Catholic authorities of the day hoped he would be in the matter of conversions.

Towards the end of his life, he told the artist Emmeline Deane that he had many close friends who were Protestants. "But, I simply have not the heart to judge them. I must leave judging to God and their consciences . . . If they trust God He will lead them to Him." When the artist asked whether God would lead them by different ways, he replied, "Yes, by different ways."[1]

Newman loved Roman Catholicism and made it quite clear that he at no stage ever contemplated returning to Anglicanism, or to any other Christian denomination, but his attitude towards his non-Roman Catholic past was one of appreciation. To the Secretary of the London Evangelisation Society, George T. Edwards, he wrote in 1887:

> . . . what should, what can, I say, but that those great and burning truths, which I learned when a boy from evangelical teaching, I have found impressed upon my heart with fresh and ever increasing force by the Holy Roman Church? That Church has added to the simple evangelicalism of my first teachers, but it has obscured, diluted, enfeebled, nothing of it — on the contrary, I have found a power, a resource, a comfort, a consolation in our Lord's divinity and atonement, in His Real Presence, in communion in His Divine

and Human Person, which all good Catholics indeed have, but which Evangelical Christians have but faintly.[2]

He never forgot those to whom he had ministered in St Clement's parish and at St Mary's, Oxford. He spoke of the deep piety and love of the Scriptures he had found there. Most of the people had not been cultured but he remembered them with affection and reverence; the memory of them could even reduce him to tears at times, as he recalled their names.

Newman did not try to rush people into belief, or into the Roman Catholic Church. He spoke to them of the need to search sincerely for the truth and to pray for light and guidance:

> Be convinced in your reason that the Catholic Church is a teacher sent to you from God, and it is enough. I do not wish you to join her, till you are. If you are half convinced, pray for full conviction, and wait till you have it. It is better indeed to come quickly, but better slowly than carelessly; and sometimes, as the proverb goes, the more haste, the worse speed. Only make yourselves sure that the delay is not from any fault of yours, which you can remedy.[3]

Newman saw understanding as the remedy for prejudice: prejudice arose from ignorance of other people and their beliefs. He not only contributed greatly to the dispelling ignorance by his voluminous correspondence with both Roman Catholics and non-Roman Catholics, and by his sermons, lectures and books, but he also did everything he could to raise the intellectual level of Roman Catholics, to improve their education in the faith so that they, in turn, could help to dispel ignorance and remove prejudice in their various spheres. He encouraged Roman Catholics to be charitable and patient in their attitudes towards other Christians, and to give an example of holiness in their lives.

It was clear from the many letters he received from non-Roman Catholics that they found his writings extremely helpful. He hoped that somehow these writings would help to lead all Christians to unity. In 1868 he wrote: "Whatever tends to create a unity of heart between men of separate communions, lays the ground for advances towards a restoration of that visible unity, the absence of which among Christians is so great a triumph, and so great an advantage to the enemies of the Cross."[4]

In selecting some of his Anglican sermons for publication, Newman was anxious that the aim should be to "cultivate a unity of ethos among those who otherwise differ."[5] He told a Congregationalist that it was a "great mystery in Providence how it comes to pass that so many minds, all so earnest both in their zeal for God and their good will towards each other, nevertheless, as a matter of strict conscience, keep at a distance from each other."[6]

The good that Newman was able to do through his writings can be seen in the letters he received from non-Roman Catholics. The following are just a few of the comments:

I am not a member of the Catholic Church, but your Writings have taught me to love and

159

reverence her. I am perhaps in the position of thousands in this kingdom from whose hearts you have extracted the deadly venom of hate and sectarian malevolence.[7]

Allow me to intrude upon you for a few moments to thank you with all my heart for the good which I have received from the reading of your books, and the singing of your hymns, both in public and private devotions. Your Sermons have helped me to know my heart better than I could have done but for the help from them received; and they have been to me inspiration and guidance in my preparations to speak to others . . . I am a Methodist Minister . . .[8]

For more than five years I have had ten volumes of your Sermons upon my shelves and during that time I have profited greatly by their careful perusal . . . Permit me to acknowledge my debt to you and to thank you most sincerely for what you have taught me during these five years . . . I am a Wesleyan Minister and have not yet completed my twenty-eighth year.[9]

Although not a member of the Catholic Church — I am a Baptist — yet you have more than once been a spiritual instructor to me and have helped to dispel the clouds of doubt and the sorrows of sin which have so often gathered around my life.[10]

As a student at Spring Hill College sixteen years ago, I first became acquainted with your works, and have never since ceased to love and venerate your name . . . You will not, I feel sure, think me (though a Congregationalist) intrusive in venturing to express those sentiments . . .[11]

In Newman one finds not so much contradiction as balance. Thus, in his attitude towards other Christians, one finds a balance between respect for individual consciences, individual convictions, and a firm attachment of himself to the Roman Catholic faith. There was no watering-down of his beliefs. In 1862 and again in 1870 he wrote:

> I have not had a moment's wavering of trust in the Catholic Church since I was received into her fold. I hold, and ever have held, that her Sovereign Pontiff is the centre of unity, and the Vicar of Christ. And I ever have had, and have still, an unclouded faith in her Creed in all its articles: a supreme satisfaction in her worship, discipline, and teaching; and an eager longing, and a hope against hope, that the many dear friends whom I have left in Protestantism may be partakers in my happiness.[12]

And yet he was uncritical of aspects of Roman Catholicism such as exaggerated types of devotion; he was not content to allow ultramontanes to give the impression that their presentation of Roman Catholic beliefs was the correct one; nor did he refrain from defending openness and truth.

With regard to the latter, he spoke with prudence and care about the inspiration of Scripture when Vatican I's teaching on this endangered the freedom which Catholics had previously had relating to biblical questions. He believed that the whole of the Scripture was indeed divinely inspired in the sense that the writer wrote what God willed should be included but that the purpose was a religious one, not an historical or scientific one. The Scriptures were concerned with faith and morals. He wrote: "As to the authority of Scripture, we hold it to be, in all matters of faith and morals, divinely inspired throughout; as to its interpretation, we hold that the Church is, in faith and morals, the one infallible expounder of the inspired text."[13]

Newman considered that the problem of scriptural inspiration should remain an open question and not, as many theologians wished, a closed one which would have seriously jeopardised scholarly research. His contribution in this matter was a very valuable one and is reflected both in the *magna carta* of biblical studies, Pope Pius XII's encyclical *Divino Afflante Spiritu* (1943) and in Vatican II's documents.

Newman had no fears regarding apparent conflicts between the truths of science and of belief. Truth would, in fact, not contradict itself. He regarded education as being needed to meet the challenges presented by science and historical study to the theological and biblical claims of Christianity. Faith and science should be in harmony:

> Devotion is not a sort of finish given to the sciences; nor is science a sort of feather in the cap, if I may so express myself, an ornament and set-off to devotion. I want the intellectual layman to be religious, and the devout ecclesiastic to be intellectual.[14]

While Newman was anxious that the rights of the educated should not be denied, he was also aware that scholarly speculation could shock and scandalise those who were not used to such speculation and were not intellectually equipped to handle it:

> In certain cases there may be a duty of silence, when there is no obligation of belief. Here no question of faith comes in. We will suppose that a novel opinion about Scripture or its contents is well grounded, and that a received opinion is open to doubt, in a case in which the Church has hitherto decided nothing, so that a new question needs a new answer: here, to profess the new opinion may be abstractedly permissible, but it is not always permissible in practice. The novelty may be so startling as to require a full certainty that it is true, it may be so strange as to raise the question whether it will not unsettle ill-educated minds, — that is, though the statement is not an offence against faith, still it may be an offence against charity. It need not be heretical, yet at a particular time or place it may be so contrary to the prevalent opinion in the Catholic body, as in Galileo's case, that zeal for the supremacy of the Divine Word, deference to existing authorities, charity towards the weak and ignorant, and distrust of self, should keep a man from being impetuous or careless in circulating what nevertheless he holds to be true, and what, if indeed asked about, he cannot deny. The household of God has claims upon our tenderness in such matters which criticism and history have not.[15]

Whether or not one entirely agrees with the statement, it is certainly as relevant to the latter part of the 20th century as it was in Newman's time.

Another area in Newman's life in which one

can see a balance that is as much needed today as then is in relation to conscience and obedience to authority in the Church. Newman was certainly the champion of the rights of a person's conscience, including his own. He saw it as the soul's main guide; an inner authoritative "voice" that commends or condemns a person's thoughts and actions. One may try to ignore it or change it to suit one's feelings, but it cannot be destroyed. Newman referred to it as the "aboriginal Vicar of Christ".[16] People had been led to God through following their consciences centuries before any Pope appeared in history. When Newman was preparing to write a reply to Gladstone's article on the First Vatican Council, he was told by someone that it had been intimated that he should, in fact, write nothing about the matter. His calm reply was: "When my conscience tells me what I should do, no authority on earth can be let stand between me and my God."[17]

However, as Newman himself pointed out in strong terms, he was not advocating "private judgement" in the Protestant sense, when he defended the rights of an individual's conscience. And in Newman's life an outstanding feature is his obedience to authority. His spirit of obedience towards his bishop was exemplary as an Anglican and was the same towards the Roman Catholic hierarchy after his conversion.

Regarding prompt obedience, Newman wrote: "I never have resisted, nor can resist, the voice of a lawful Superior, speaking in his own province."[18]

He was certainly not among the ultramontanes but his whole-hearted loyalty and support for the Pope was unwavering:

> We must never murmur at that absolute rule which the Sovereign Pontiff has over us, because it is given to him by Christ, and, in obeying him, we are obeying Our Lord. We must never suffer ourselves to doubt, that, in his government of the Church, he is guided by an intelligence more than human. His yoke is the yoke of Christ, *he* has the responsibility of his own acts, not we; and to his *Lord* must he render account, not to us. Even in secular matters it is ever safe to be on his side, dangerous to be on the side of his enemies.[19]

Newman would have had no difficulty in accepting the teaching of Vatican II that "religious allegiance of mind and will" should be given to the "authentic magisterium of the Roman Pontiff, even when he is not speaking *ex cathedra* . . . The result should be a sincere adherence to the judgements which he has delivered, that complies with his manifest meaning and intention . . ." (*Lumen Gentium*, 25)

When an Oratorian took unkindly to his book having to be censored, Newman wrote to the man's superior: "He is only half a man if he can't put his book into the fire when told by authority."[20]

There were those who considered that Newman was guilty of "Modernism". However, he was firmly defended by none other than Pope St Pius X himself. Writing in 1908 to the Bishop of Limerick, the Pope said:

We would have you know that your pamphlet, in which you show that the writings of Cardinal Newman, so far from differing from our Encyclical Letter *Pascendi*, are in closest harmony with it, has our strongest approval. You could not indeed have done better service alike to the cause of truth and to the eminent merit of the man.[21]

Newman's attitude towards obedience to ecclesiastical authority was rooted in his trust in Divine Providence, and that all would be well in the end. In 1859 he wrote:

I have always preached that things which are *really* useful, still are done, according to God's will, at one time, not at another — and that, if you attempt at a wrong time, what is in itself right, you perhaps become a heretic or schismatic. What I may aim at may be real and good, but it may be God's will it should be done a hundred years later.[22]

Prophetic words. Many of Newman's ideas came to fruition at the second Vatican Council which opened in 1962.

Notes

[1] Recollections of Emmeline Deane. *CP* Vol. VII, p. 2502.
[2] Letter, 24/2/1887. *LD* XXXI, p. 189.
[3] *Discourses to Mixed Congregations*, No. XI, p. 234.
[4] Letter to H. Allon, 28/1/1868. *LD* XXIV, p. 22.
[5] Letter to W. J. Copeland, 13/10/1877. *LD* XXVIII, p. 248.
[6] Letter to G. Slatyer Barrett, 13/10/1882. *LD* XXX, pp. 137–138.

[7] From letter to Newman, 15/8/1882, *CP* Vol. XII, p. 4193. (Name of sender deleted from letter).

[8] Letter from R. Gray, 31/10/1882. *CP* Vol. XII, p. 4201.

[9] Letter from Thomas Harrison, 9/1/1886. *CP* Vol. XII, p. 4292.

[10] Letter from A. W. Field, 15/1/1887. *CP* Vol. XII, p. 4334.

[11] Letter from J. H. Robison, 20/2/1887. *CP* Vol. XII, p. 4353.

[12] Letter to S. Walshaw, 11/4/1870. *LD* XXV, p. 90.

[13] *CP* Vol. VIII, p. 2850.

[14] *Sermons Preached on Various Occasions*, No. I, p. 13.

[15] *CP* Vol. VIII, pp. 2852–2854.

[16] *CP* Vol. VIII, p. 2763.

[17] *CP* Vol. VI, p. 2107.

[18] Letter to E. Healy Thompson, 29/5/1859. *LD* XIX, p. 150.

[19] *Sermons Preached on Various Occasions*, No. XV, p. 286.

[20] Letter to R. A. Coffin, 27/10/1848. *LD* XII, p. 311.

[21] *CP* Vol. IX, p. 3324.

[22] Letter to H. Wilberforce, 17/7/1859. *LD* XIX, p. 179.

Section III

Words from Newman

13

Words from Newman

. . .The whole duty of a Christian is made up of these two parts, Faith and Obedience: "looking unto Jesus", the Divine Object as well as Author of our faith, and acting according to His Will.[1]

Remember that we are never more than instruments of God; we must put our hand in His and let Him lead us. His will is so mysterious. We must say "Thy will be done." He will never forget us. He never forgets, even when it seems most that we are forgotten, we are not forgotten. He will lead us if we trust ourselves to Him.[2]

One must submit oneself to God's loving Will — and be quieted by faith that what He wills for us is best.[3]

God does not require of us impossibilities — if we are perplexed, we *are* perplexed. What is our duty *under* the perplexity? Is it not to wait on Him?[4]

If you are conscious that your hearts are hard and are desirous that they should be softened, do not despair. All things are possible to you through God's grace. Come to him for the will and the power to do that to which he calls you.[5]

Those who make comfort the great subject of their preaching seem to mistake the end of their ministry. *Holiness* is the great end. There must be struggle and a trial here. Comfort is a cordial, but no one drinks cordials from morning to night.[6]

You must either conquer the world, or the world will conquer you. You must be either master or slave. Take your part then, and "stand fast in the liberty wherewith Christ hath made us free." (Gal 5:1)[7]

We advance by yielding; we rise by falling; we conquer by suffering; we persuade by silence; we become rich by bountifulness; we inherit the earth through meekness; we gain comfort through mourning; we earn glory by penitence and prayer.[8]

Pride, sensuality, selfishness, worldliness, distrust of God . . . are the real enemies of religion, and as these are the ruling spirit in every age of the world, the form which their hostility to it takes, in an ignorant age is superstition, in an inquiring age is scepticism.[9]

Christianity has never yet had experience of a world simply irreligious.[10]

Truth has a power of its own, which makes its way — it is stronger than error.[11]

It is a thought I have made much use of for

more than fifty years, that, so great is the power of prayer and the promise made to it, that I believe it to be successful in a particular case, though there be nothing in the visible disposition of things to countenance that belief, or when, rather, sight is in opposition to that belief.[12]

Make the Holy Family your home, to which you may turn from all the sorrow and care of the world, and find a solace, a compensation and a refuge.[13]

The best preparation for loving the world at large, and loving it duly and wisely, is to cultivate an intimate friendship and affection towards those who are immediately about us.[14]

Nothing is more difficult than to realise that every man has a distinct soul, that every one of all the millions who live or have lived, is as whole and independent a being in himself, as if there were no one else in the whole world but he.[15]

Christ has done the whole work of redemption for us; and yet it is no contradiction to say that something remains for us to do: we have to take the redemption offered to us, and that taking involves a work. We have to apply his grace to our own souls, and that application implies pain, trial, and toil. He has suffered and conquered, and those who become partakers in Him, undergo in their own persons the shadow and likeness of that passion and victory.[16]

May the Lord support us all the day long, till the shades lengthen and the evening comes, and the busy world is hushed, and the fever of life is over, and our work is done. Then in his mercy, may he give us a safe lodging, and a holy rest, and peace at the last.[17]

We are not sent into this world for nothing; we are not born at random; we are not here, that we may go to bed at night, and get up in the morning, toil for our bread, eat and drink, laugh and joke, sin when we have a mind, and reform when we are tired of sinning, rear a family and die . . . He has an end for each of us; we are all equal in His sight, and we are placed in our different ranks and stations, not to get what we can out of them for ourselves, but to labour in them for Him.[18]

All the peculiarity of a Christian consists in his preferring God and his neighbour to *self*, — in self-denial for the sake of God and his brethren.[19]

A rigorous self-denial is a chief duty . . . it may be considered the test whether we are Christ's disciples. Whether we are living in a mere dream, which we mistake for Christian faith and obedience, or are really and truly awake, alive, living the day — on our road heavenwards.[20]

They (then) watch and wait for their Lord who are tender and sensitive in their devotion towards Him; who feed on the thought of Him, hang on His words; live in His smile, and thrive

174

and grow under his hand. They are eager for His approval, quick in catching His meaning, jealous for His honour. They see Him in all things, expect Him in all events . . .[21]

God gives His Holy Spirit to us silently; and the silent duties of every day (it may be humbly hoped) are blest to the sufficient sanctification of thousands, whom the world knows not of. The Blessed Virgin is a memorial of this; and it is consoling as well as instructive to know it.[22]

How is our devotion to Christ shown? Ordinarily, not in great matters, not in giving up house and lands for His sake, but in making little sacrifices which the world would ridicule, if it knew of them.[23]

Man is not sufficient for his own happiness; he is not happy except the Presence of God be with him.[24]

To hear some men speak (I mean men who scoff at religion), it might be thought we never acted on Faith or Trust, except in religious matters; whereas we are acting on trust every hour of our lives.[25]

The great rule of our conduct is to take things as they come. He who goes out of his way as shrinking from the varieties of human life which meet him, has weak faith, or a strangely perverted conscience — he wants elevation of mind. The true Christian rejoices in those earthly things which give joy, but in such a way as not to care for them when they go. For no blessings does he care much, except those which are immortal, knowing that he shall receive all such again in the world to come.[26]

God beholds thee individually, whoever thou art. He "calls thee by name." He sees thee, and understands thee, as He made thee. He knows what is in thee, all thy own peculiar feelings and thoughts, thy dispositions and likings, thy strength and thy weakness. He views thee in thy day of rejoicing, and thy day of sorrow. He sympathizes in thy hopes and thy temptations. He interests Himself in all thy anxieties and remembrances, all the risings and fallings of thy spirit. He has numbered the very hairs of thy head and the cubits of thy stature. He compasses thee round and bears thee in His arms; He takes thee up and sets thee down. He notes thy very countenance, whether smiling or in tears, whether healthful or sickly. He looks tenderly upon thy hands and thy feet; He hears thy voice, the beating of thy heart, and thy very breathing. Thou dost not love thyself better than He loves thee. Thou canst not shrink from pain more than He dislikes thy bearing it; and if he puts it on thee, it is as thou wilt put it on thyself, if thou art wise, for a greater good afterwards. Thou art not only His creature (though for the very sparrows He has a care, and pitied the "much cattle" of Nineveh), thou art man redeemed and sanctified, His adopted son, favoured with a portion of that glory and blessedness which flows from Him everlastingly unto the Only-begotten . . . Thou art chosen to be His, even above thy fellows who dwell in the East and South. Thou wast one of those for whom Christ offered up His last prayer, and sealed it with His precious blood. What a thought is this, a thought almost too great for our faith! [27]

There is no end of God's power; it is inexhaustible. Let there be no end to our faith. Let us not be startled at what we are called on to believe; let us still be on the look out. Some people are slow to believe the miracles ascribed to the Saints. Now we know that such miracles are not part of the *faith*; they have no place in the Creed. And some are reported on better evidence than others. Some may be true, and others not so certainly true. Others again may be true, but not miracles. But still why should they be *surprised* to hear of miracles? Are they beyond the power of God, and is not God present with the Saints, and has He not wrought miracles of old? Are miracles a new thing? There is no reason to be surprised; on the contrary, because in the Sacrifice of the Mass He works daily the most wonderful of miracles at the word of the priest. If, then, He does daily a miracle greater than any that can be named, why should we be surprised to hear reports of His doing other and lesser miracles now and then? [28]

Can any state be more fearful than that of an immortal being, who is to live for ever, attempting to live on mortal food, and having no relish for that immortal food which alone is its true nourishment? [29]

177

The whirl and dance of worldly matters is but like the whirling of chaff or dust, nothing comes of it; it lasts through the day, but it is not to be found in the evening. And yet how many immortal souls spend their lives in nothing better than making themselves giddy with this whirl of politics, of party, or religious opinion, or money getting, of which nothing can ever come.[30]

No sinner, ever so odious, but may become a Saint; no Saint, ever so exalted, but has been, or might have been, a sinner.[31]

In those [Saints] who have never sinned gravely love is so contemplative as almost to resolve itself into the sanctity of God himself; in those, on the contrary, in whom it dwells as a principle of recovery, it is so full of devotion, of zeal, of activity, and good works, that it gives a visible character to their history, and is ever associating itself with our thoughts of them.[32]

We do not know what sin is, because we do not know what God is; we have no standard with which to compare it, till we know what God is. Only God's glories, His perfections, His holiness, His majesty, His beauty, can teach us by the contrast how to think of sin; and since we do not see God here, till we see Him, we cannot form a just judgement of what sin is; till we enter heaven, we must take what God tells us of sin, mainly on faith.[33]

Grace has vanquished nature; that is the whole history of the Saints. Salutary thought for those who are tempted to pride themselves in what they do, and what they are; wonderful news for those who sorrowfully recognise in their hearts the vast difference that exists between them and the Saints; and joyful news, when men hate sin, and wish to escape from its miserable yoke, yet are tempted to think it impossible![34]

The special peril of the time before us is the spread of that plague of infidelity, that the Apostles and our Lord Himself have predicted as the worst calamity of the last times of the Church. And at least a shadow, a typical image of the last times is coming over the world. I do not mean to presume to say that this is the last time, but that it has had the evil prerogative of being like that more terrible season, when it is said that the elect themselves will be in danger of falling away.[35]

We must surrender to Him all we have, all we are. We must keep nothing back. We must present to Him as captive prisoners with whom He may do what He will, our soul and body, our reason, our judgement, our affections, our imagination, our tastes, our appetite. The great thing is to *subdue* ourselves; but as to the particular form in which the great precept of self-conquest and self-surrender is to be expressed, that depends on the person himself, and on the time or place. What is good for one age or person is not good for another.[36]

It is by coming daily into His presence that

by degrees we find ourselves awed by that presence and able to believe and obey him. Therefore if anyone desires illumination to know God's will, as well as strength to do it, let him come to Mass daily, if he possibly can. At least let him present himself daily before the Blessed Sacrament, and, as it were, offer his heart to his Incarnate Saviour, presenting it as a reasonable offering to be influenced, changed, and sanctified under the eye and by the grace of the Eternal Son. And let him every now and then through the day make some short prayer or ejaculation to the Lord and Saviour, and again to His Blessed Mother, the immaculate most Blessed Virgin Mary, or again to his Guardian Angel, or to his Patron Saint. Let him now and then collect his mind and place himself, as if in heaven, in the presence of God; as if before God's throne; let him fancy he sees the All-Holy Lamb of God, which taketh away the sin of the world. These are the means by which, with God's grace, he will be able in the course of time to soften his heart — not all at once, but by degrees; not by his own power or wisdom, but by the grace of God blessing his endeavour. Thus it is that saints have begun. They have begun by these little things, and so become at length saints. They were not saints all at once, but by little and little. And so we, who are not saints, must still proceed by the same road; by lowliness, patience, trust in God, recollection that we are in His presence, and thankfulness for His mercies.[37]

180

The holy Fathers of the Church tell us again and again that our Lady was more blessed in doing God's will than in being His Mother. She was blessed in two ways. She was blessed in being His Mother; she was blessed in being filled with the spirit of faith and obedience. And the latter blessedness was the greater . . . St Augustine says: "More blessed was Mary in receiving the faith of Christ, than in receiving the flesh of Christ." In like manner St Elizabeth says to her at the Visitation, "*Beata es quae credidisti* — Blessed art thou who didst believe"; and St Chrysostom goes as far as to say that she would not have been blessed, even though she had borne Christ in the body, unless she had heard the word of God and kept it.[38]

What an unexpected sight, at the last day and public judgement to be present at that revelation of all hearts! How different persons will then seem from what they seem now! How will the last be first and first last! Then those whom the world looked up to will be brought low, and those who were little esteemed will be exalted. Then will it be found who are the real movers in the world's affairs; those who sustained the cause of the Church or who influenced the fortunes of empires were not the great and powerful, not those whose names are known in the world; but the humble, despised followers of the Lamb, the meek saint, the man full of prayer and good works whom the world passed by; the hidden band of saintly witnesses, whose voice day by day ascended to Christ; the sufferers who seemed to be living for nothing; the poor whom the proud world thought but an offence and a nuisance. When that day comes, may it reveal good for each of you, my brethren.[39]

If St Peter could say at the Transfiguration, "It is good to be here", much more shall we have cause to say so when we see the face of God. For then we shall be like our Lord Himself, we shall have glorified bodies, as He had then and has now. We shall have put off flesh and blood, and receive our bodies at the last day, the same indeed, but incorruptible, spiritual bodies, which will be able to see and enjoy the presence of God in a way beyond the three Apostles [Peter, James and John] in the days of their mortality. Then the envious malignant spirit will be cast out, and we shall have nothing to fear, nothing to be perplexed at, for the Lord God shall lighten us, and encompass us, and we shall be in perfect security and peace. Then we shall look back upon this world, and the trials and temptations which are past, and what thankfulness, what joy will not rise within us — and we shall look forward, and this one thought will be upon us, that this blessedness is to last for ever.[40]

Notes

[1] *PPS* Vol. 2, Sermon XIV, p. 153.

[2] Recollections of Emmeline Deane, *CP* Vol. VII, p. 2501.

[3] Letter to Miss Munro, 21/10/1875. *LD* XXVI, p. 376.

[4] Letter to W. C. A. Maclaurin, 8/10/1840. *CP* Vol. III, p. 1032.

[5] *Catholic Sermons*, pp. 52–53.

[6] *Autobiographical Writings*, p. 172.

[7] *Sermons on Subjects of the Day*, Sermon VIII, p. 111.

[8] Ibid., Sermon XII, p. 162.

[9] *The Theological Papers of John Henry Newman on Faith and Certainty*, OUP, 1976, p. 8.

[10] *Catholic Sermons*, p. 123.

[11] Letter to W. J. Copeland, 20/4/1873. *LD* XXVI, p. 294.

[12] Letter to William Philip Gordon, 28/2/1876. *LD* XXVIII, p. 34.

[13] *Addresses to Cardinal Newman with his replies*, edited by William Neville, Longmans Green, London, 1905, p. 228.

[14] *PPS* Vol. 2, Sermon V, pp. 52–53.

[15] *PPS* Vol. 4, Sermon VI, pp. 80–81.

[16] *Sermons on Subjects of the Day*, Sermon XII, p. 161.

[17] *Sermons on Subjects of the Day*, Sermon XX, p. 307.

[18] *Discourses to Mixed Congregations*, No. VI, p. 111.

[19] *Sermons on Subjects of the Day*, Sermon II, p. 23.

[20] *PPS* Vol. I, Sermon V, p. 66.

[21] *Sermons Preached on Various Occasions*, Sermon III, p. 35.

[22] *PPS* Vol. 2, Sermon XII, p. 136.

[23] *PPS* Vol. 3, Sermon XV, p. 210.

[24] *Sermons on Subjects of the Day*, Sermon XXI, p. 312.

[25] *PPS* Vol. I, Sermon XV, p. 191.

[26] *PPS* Vol. I, Sermon XXV, p. 333.

[27] *PPS* Vol. 3, Sermon IX, pp. 124–125.

[28] *Catholic Sermons*, pp. 26–27.

[29] Ibid., p. 86.

[30] Ibid., p. 39.

[31] *Discourses to Mixed Congregations*, No. III, p. 57.

[32] Ibid., No. IV, p. 72.

[33] Ibid., No. II, p. 33.

[34] Ibid., No. III, p. 49.

[35] *Catholic Sermons*, p. 121.

[36] Ibid., pp. 67–68.

[37] Ibid., pp. 53–54.

[38] Ibid., pp. 93–94.

[39] Ibid., p. 41–42.

[40] Ibid., pp. 90–91.

Select Bibliography

Cameron, J. M., *John Henry Newman* (No. 72 in the series 'Writers and Their Work'), Longmans, Green and Co., London, 1956

Campion, E., *John Henry Newman — Friends, Allies, Bishops, Catholics*, Dove Communications, Melbourne, 1980

Chadwick, O., *Newman* (Past Masters series), Oxford University Press, Oxford, 1987

Dessain, C. S., *Newman's Spiritual Themes*, Veritas, Dublin, 1977

Faber, G., *Oxford Apostles*, Faber and Faber, London, 1974

Graef, H., *God and Myself — The Spirituality of John Henry Newman,* Peter Davies, London, 1967

Newman, J. H., *Apologia Pro Vita Sua*, J. M. Dent, London, 1938
— *Autobiographical Writings*, edited and introduced by H. Tristram, Sheed and Ward, London, 1956
— *Catholic Sermons of Cardinal Newman*, Burns & Oates, 1957
— *Discourses addressed to Mixed Congregations*, Burns & Oates, London, 1881
— *Historical Sketches*, Longmans, Green and Co., London, 1885
— *Lectures on Certain Difficulties felt by Anglicans in submitting to the Catholic Church*, Longmans, Green and Co., London, 1897
— *Lectures on the Present Position of Catholics in England*, Burns & Oates, London, 1872
— *Letter to the Rev. E. B. Pusey DD on his recent Eirenicon, A*, Longmans, Green, Reader and Dyer, London, 1866
— *Letters and Diaries of John Henry Newman* Ed. at Birmingham Oratory by C. S. Dessain *et al*, Nelson and Oxford, 1961
— *Loss and Gain*, Oxford University Press, Oxford, 1986
— *Meditations and Devotions*, Burns & Oates, London 1964
— *Parochial and Plain Sermons*, (8 volumes), Rivingtons, London, 1869–1882
— *Sermons on Subjects of the Day*, Rivingtons, London, 1885
— *Sermons preached before the University of Oxford*, Rivingtons, London, 1884
— *Sermons preached on Various Occasions*, Burns & Oates, London, 1881.
— *Verses on Various Occasions*, Burns & Oates, 1883

Stanford D. and Spark M., editors, *Letters of John Henry Newman*,
     Peter Owen, London, 1957

Trevor M., *Newman's Journey*, Collins (Fontana), London, 1974

Wilson A., *Blessed Dominic Barberi*, Sands & Co, London, 1967

Young G. M., *Victorian England — Portrait of an Age*, Oxford
     University Press, London, 1960

Zeno Dr., *John Henry Newman — His Inner Life*, Ignatius Press,
     San Francisco, 1987

IMAGES OF HOLINESS

Series Editor: Felicity O'Brien, B.A.

Consultant Editor: Fr Paul Molinari, S.J.,
Professor of Spiritual Theology at the Gregorian
University, Rome; Chairman of the College of
Postulators.*

Postulators promote the causes of candidates for beatification or canonization.

THE CHEERFUL GIVER
Margaret Sinclair

by Felicity O'Brien

Margaret Ann Sinclair was born on 29th March 1900, in Edinburgh. For twenty-three years she lived an ordinary family life reaching out to people with her constant serenity and cheerfulness. She joined the Poor Clares in 1923, and died of tuberculosis at the age of twenty-five.

Margaret's holiness was already manifest among her contemporaries. She is an outstanding example and source of inspiration for Christians today.

FELICITY O'BRIEN is a freelance writer. For a number of years she worked with the Catholic weekly, The Universe. *From there she moved on to take charge of the publications department of the Independent Broadcasting Authority. She lives in Kent.*

NO GREATER LOVE
Damien apostle of the lepers

by John Milsome

This is the story of a man – Joseph de Veuster, better known as Father Damien, "the hero of Molokai" – who devoted his life to the welfare of the lepers on the island of Molokai, in the Pacific Ocean. The conditions on the island were daunting. The lepers lived in squalor and misery. Being a foreigner he was not at once welcomed by the lepers. His "ragged honesty, generosity and mirth" however, won them over as friends.

What is Damien's relevance for us today? Basically three things: fidelity to one's calling, dedication to a worthy cause and compassion for the underprivileged and outcasts of the society.

Robert Louis Stevenson wrote of Damien: "It was his part, by one striking act of martyrdom, to direct all men's eyes on this distressful country. At a blow and with the price of his life, he made the place illustrious and public... If ever any man brought reforms and died to bring them, it was he." This is the challenge unfolded in the pages of *No Greater Love*.

JOHN MILSOME was born in Pinner, Middlesex. He trained as a teacher and his main interest outside teaching was his writing career. The completion of No Greater Love *was sealed with his premature death.*